THREE CHALLENGES TO ETHICS

Environmentalism, Feminism, and Multiculturalism

James P. Sterba

New York   Oxford
Oxford University Press
2001

Oxford University Press

Oxford   New York
Athens   Auckland   Bangkok   Bogotá   Buenos Aires   Calcutta
Cape Town   Chennai   Dar es Salaam   Delhi   Florence   Hong Kong   Istanbul
Karachi   Kuala Lumpur   Madrid   Melbourne   Mexico City   Mumbai
Nairobi   Paris   São Paulo   Singapore   Taipei   Tokyo   Toronto   Warsaw

and associated companies in
Berlin   Ibadan

Copyright © 2001 by Oxford University Press, Inc.

Published by Oxford University Press, Inc.
198 Madison Avenue, New York, New York 10016
http://www.oup-usa.org

Oxford is a registered trademark of Oxford University Press

Library of Congress Cataloging-in-Publication Data

Sterba, James P.
    Three challenges to ethics : environmentalism, feminism, and multiculturalism / James
P. Sterba.
        p. cm.
    Includes bibliographical references and index.
    ISBN 0-19-512475-8 (cloth : acid-free paper)—ISBN 0-19-512476-6 (paper : acid-free paper)
    1. Ethics. 2. Feminist ethics. 3. Multiculturalism. 4. Environmental ethics. I. Title.
BJ1012.S69 2000
170—dc21   99-054881

Printing (last digit): 9 8 7 6 5 4 3 2 1

Printed in the United States of America
on acid-free paper

V C gift

CONTENTS

Preface   v

1   INTRODUCTION
Traditional Ethics   1

2   ENVIRONMENTALISM
The Human Bias in Traditional Ethics
and How to Correct It   27

3   FEMINISM
The Masculine Bias in Traditional Ethics
and How to Correct It   51

4   MULTICULTURALISM
The Western Bias in Traditional Ethics
and How to Correct It   77

5   CONCLUSION
A Peacemaking Way of Doing
Philosophy   105

Notes   119
Bibliography   143
Index   151

PREFACE

In this book, I argue that traditional ethics has yet to face up to three important challenges that come from environmentalism, feminism, and multiculturalism. Failure to meet these challenges has meant that no matter how successful traditional ethics has been at dealing with the problems it recognizes, it has as yet failed to deal with the possibility that its solutions to these problems are biased in favor of humans, biased in favor of men, and biased in favor of Western culture. Failure to deal with these challenges has clearly put the justification for traditional ethics into question. Accordingly, those concerned with the justification of traditional ethics have no alternative but to try to determine how these challenges can be met. This is what I try to do in this book.

As you would expect, in writing this book, I have benefited from the comments of many different people. In particular, I would like to thank some of my colleagues at Notre Dame: David O'Connor, Philip Quinn, Kristin Shrader-Frechette, David Solomon, and Paul Weithman. I also thank David Benatar of the University of Cape Town, South Africa, Joan Callahan of the University of Kentucky, Joseph DesJardins of St. John's College, Bernard Gert of Dartmouth College, Sandra Harding of UCLA, Virginia Held of the City University of New York, Alison Jaggar of the University of Colorado, Maria Morales of Florida State University, Brian Penrose and Michael Pendlebury of the University of Witwaterstrand, South Africa, Sabine Roeser of the Free University of Amsterdam, Ruth Sample of the University of New Hampshire, Laurie Shrage of California Polytechnic State University, Walter Sinnott-Armstrong of Dartmouth College, Mary Ann Warren of San Francisco State University, Karen Warren of Macalester College, Peter Wenz of the University of Illinois at Springfield, and especially my partner and fellow philosopher, Janet Kourany. I would also like to thank the editors of *Ethics, Environmental Ethics,* and Cambridge University Press for permission to draw on previously published work, and the University of Notre Dame for financial support.

1

INTRODUCTION

Traditional Ethics

Traditional ethics admits of a great deal of diversity. Some of its practitioners are subjectivists and relativists while others are objectivists and universalists. Some seek to show that morality is rationally required while others are content to show that morality is just rationally permissible, even if this entails that egoism and amorality are rationally permissible as well. Among its practitioners are Aristotelians, who want us to live a virtuous life, Kantians, who want us to do our duty, and utilitarians, who want us to maximize utility.

Yet despite its diversity and its openness to a range of solutions to the central problems it recognizes, traditional ethics has yet to face up to three important challenges. These challenges come from environmentalism, feminism, and multiculturalism.

1. Environmentalism maintains that there is a human bias in ethics and purports to show how to correct it.[1]
2. Feminism maintains that there is a masculine bias in ethics and purports to show how to correct it.
3. Multiculturalism maintains that there is a Western bias in ethics and purports to show how to correct it.

That traditional ethics has not paid attention to these challenges has meant that no matter how successful it has been at dealing with the problems it has recognized, it still has failed to deal with the possibility that its solutions to these problems are biased in favor of humans, biased in favor of men, and biased in favor of Western culture. Failure to deal with these challenges has clearly put the justification for traditional ethics into question. Thus, those concerned with the justification of traditional ethics have no alternative but to try to determine how these challenges can be met. To set the stage for dealing with these challenges, I propose in this chapter to consider three of the main problems dealt with in traditional ethics: the problem of relativism (Is morality relative?), the problem of rationality (Is morality rationally required?), and the problem of practical requirements (What does morality require?). By providing solutions to each of these problems, I hope to show that traditional ethics has sufficient resources for addressing the challenges of environmentalism, feminism, and multiculturalism. I will then address each of these challenges in turn in the chapters that follow.

The Problem of Relativism: Is Morality Relative?

Many people think that morality is a matter of opinion and that what is right for you may be wrong for me even if we are similarly situated. Such people are moral relativists, and they take their view to be amply supported by the diverse moral views held in different societies as well as by the level of moral disagreement that exists within any given society. In my own society, there is presently radical disagreement over such issues as abortion, welfare, homosexuality, and humanitarian intervention. Yet these disagreements seem to pall when my own society is compared with other societies that presently condone infanticide, polygamy, and even cannibalism.

Nevertheless, in order for moral relativists to draw support from this moral diversity, they must be able to show that the same act could be both right and wrong—right for one society, group, or individual, and wrong for some other society, group, or individual. Frequently, however, the act that is condemned by one society, group, or individual is not the same act that is sanctioned by another society, group, or individual. For example, the voluntary euthanasia that is sanctioned by Eskimos as a transition to what they take to be a happier existence for their aged members is significantly different from the euthanasia that the AMA opposes, which does not assume a happier afterlife.[2] Likewise, when the Nuers gently lay their deformed infants in the river because they believe that such infants are baby hippos accidentally born to humans, their action is significantly different from the infanticide that most people condemn.[3] Even in the case of abortion, what some people judge to be right (permissible) and what other people judge to be wrong (impermissible) would not appear to be the same act, because of the different views that people hold with respect to the moral status of the fetus. Those opposing abortion usually claim that the fetus is a full-fledged human person with the same right to life as you or I, while those favoring abortion usually deny that the fetus has this status.[4]

Yet even when the same act is being compared, in order for it to be right for a person to do, it must be possible for that person, following his or her best deliberation, to come to judge the act as right. Acts that are inaccessible to people's best judgment (like avoiding carcinogens in the Middle Ages) are not acts that could be morally right for them to do because morality requires a certain accessibility.[5] Accordingly, when we evaluate people's moral judgments in the context in which they formed them, it will sometimes be the case that we will recognize that they couldn't have arrived at the judgments that we think are morally right. If so, their judgments would not relevantly conflict with our own, even if what they think is right is not what we think is right—for example, as in the need for cleanliness in medical operations.

Of course, this is not to suggest that what we think is right for us to do is necessarily right for us to do. After all, we could be mistaken. It is only to suggest that if we are moral agents capable of moral deliberation, any discrepancy between what is right for us to do and what we think is right for us to do must be explained in terms of some kind of past or present failure on our part to follow our best deliberation with regard to the opportunities that are available to us. If it is going to make any sense to say that something is right for us to do, knowledge of that fact must somehow be accessible to us, so that any discrepancy between what is right for us to do and what we think is right for us to do must somehow be traceable to a failure on our part to deliberate wisely.[6] Consequently, in order for moral relativism to draw support from the existing moral diversity, there must be acts that are sufficiently accessible to people's moral deliberation such that the same act is judged right by some people using their best moral judgment, and judged wrong by other people using their best moral judgment.

But even this is not enough. Moral relativism must also tell us what morality is supposed to be relative *to*.[7] Is it to be relative to the common beliefs of a society, to those of a smaller group, or to those of just any individual, or could it be relative to any of these? If it could be relative to any of these, any act (e.g., contract killing) could be wrong from the point of view of some particular society, right from the point of view of some subgroup of that society (e.g., the Mafia), and wrong again from the point of view of some particular member of that society or subgroup. But if this is the case, individuals would not have any reasonable grounds for deciding what they ought to do, all things considered.[8]

Yet even supposing that some particular reference group could be shown to be preferable (e.g., the reference group of one's own society), problems remain. First, in deciding what to do, should we simply ask what the members of our appropriate reference group think ought to be done? But if everyone in our reference group did that, we would all be waiting for everyone else to decide, and so no one would decide what ought to be done. Or we might construe moral relativism to be a second-order theory that requires that the members of our appropriate reference group first decide on some other grounds what is right and then take a vote. If a majority or a consensus emerges from such a vote, then that is what is right, all things considered. So interpreted, "moral relativism" would have some merit as a theory of collective decision making, but it clearly would require some yet-to-be-determined nonrelativist grounds for first-order moral judgments, and so it would not essentially be a relativist theory at all.

Second, the very claim that morality should be specified relativistically is not itself a relativistic claim. Rather, it claims to be a truth for all times and places. But how can this be possible? Shouldn't the truth of relativism itself be assertible as a relativistic claim? One might maintain that while moral judgments are relativistic, the thesis of moral relativism is not itself a moral claim and, hence, need not be relativistic. But if truth is not relativistic, why should we think that the good is relativistic?

In sum, moral relativism as an account of moral judgments faces a number of difficulties. First, it is difficult for moral relativists to show that amid the existing moral diversity there are acts that are sufficiently accessible to people's moral deliberation such that the same act is judged right by some and wrong by others when all are following their best moral deliberation. Second, it is difficult for moral relativists to specify the appropriate reference group from which morality is to be determined. Third, even assuming that the appropriate reference group can be determined, it is difficult for moral relativists to explain why their theory is not committed to some nonrelativist account of at least first-order moral judgments. Last, it is difficult for moral relativists to explain why they are committed to a nonrelativist account of truth.

Yet while these difficulties obviously render moral relativism an implausible theory, they do not completely defeat it in the absence of a better nonrelativistic account of morality. In such an account, it would be helpful to show that morality is rationally required and not just rationally permissible, which leads naturally to the second problem of traditional ethics that I proposed to take up.

The Problem of Rationality: Is Morality Rationally Required?

The main obstacle to showing that morality is rationally required is ethical egoism, which denies the priority of morality over self-interest. Basically, ethical egoism takes two forms: individual ethical egoism and universal ethical egoism. The basic principle of individual ethical egoism is:

> Everyone ought to do what is in the overall self-interest of just one particular individual.

The basic principle of universal ethical egoism is:

> Everyone ought to do what is in his or her overall self-interest.

Obviously, the practical requirements of these two forms of egoism would conflict significantly with the practical requirements of morality. How then can we show that the practical requirements of morality are rationally preferable to those of egoism?

Individual Ethical Egoism

In individual ethical egoism, all practical requirements are derived from the overall interests of just one particular individual. Let's call that individual Gladys. Because Gladys's interests constitute the sole basis for determining practical requirements according to individual ethical egoism, there should be no problem of inconsistent requirements, assuming, of course, that Gladys's own particular interests are in harmony. The crucial problem for individual ethical egoism, however, is justifying that only Gladys's interests should count in determining practical requirements. Individual ethical egoism must provide at least some reason for accepting that view. Otherwise, it would be irrational to accept the theory. But what reason or reasons could serve this function? Clearly, it will not do to cite some characteristic Gladys shares with other persons because whatever justification such a characteristic would provide for favoring Gladys's interests, it would also provide for favoring the interests of those other persons. Nor will it do to cite as a reason some unique characteristic of Gladys's, such as knowing all of Shakespeare's writings by heart, because such a characteristic involves a comparative element; consequently, others with similar characteristics, like knowing some or most of Shakespeare by heart, would still have some justification, although a proportionally lesser justification, for having their interests favored. But again the proposed characteristic would not justify favoring only Gladys's interests.

A similar objection could be raised if a unique relational characeristic were proposed as a reason for Gladys's special status—

such as that Gladys is Seymour's wife. Because other persons would have similar but not identical relational characteristics, similar but not identical reasons would hold for them. Nor will it do to argue that the reason for Gladys's special status is not the particular unique traits that she possesses, but rather the mere fact that she has unique traits. The same would hold true of everyone else. Every individual has unique traits. If recourse to unique traits is dropped and Gladys claims that she is special simply because she is herself and wants to further her own interests, every other person could claim the same.[9]

For the individual ethical egoist to argue that the same or similar reasons do *not* hold for other people with the same or similar characteristics as those of Gladys, she must explain *why* they do not hold. It must always be possible to understand how a characteristic serves as a reason in one case but not in another. If no explanation can be provided, and in the case of individual ethical egoism none has been forthcoming, the proposed characteristic either serves as a reason in both cases or does not serve as a reason at all.

Universal Ethical Egoism

Unfortunately, these objections to individual ethical egoism do not work against universal ethical egoism because the latter does provide a reason why the egoist should be concerned simply about maximizing his or her own interests. The reason is simply that the egoist is herself and wants to further her own interests. The individual ethical egoist could not recognize such a reason without giving up his view, but the universal ethical egoist is willing and able to universalize her claim and recognize that everyone has a similar justification for adopting universal ethical egoism.

Accordingly, the objections that typically have been raised against universal ethical egoism take a different tack and attempt to show that the view is fundamentally inconsistent. For the purpose of evaluating these objections, let's consider the case of Gary Gyges, an otherwise normal human being who, for reasons of personal gain, has embezzled $1,000,000 while working at People's

National Bank, and is in the process of escaping to a South Sea island where he will be able to live a pleasant life protected by the local authorities and untroubled by any qualms of conscience. Suppose that Hedda Hawkeye, a coworker, knows that Gyges has been embezzling money from the bank and is about to escape. Suppose, further, that it is in Hawkeye's overall self-interest to prevent Gyges from escaping with the embezzled money because she will be generously rewarded for doing so by being appointed vice president of the bank. Given that it is in Gyges's overall self-interest to escape with embezzled money, it now appears that we can derive a contradiction from the following:

1. Gyges ought to escape with the embezzled money.
2. Hawkeye ought to prevent Gyges from escaping with the embezzled money.
3. By preventing Gyges from escaping with the embezzled money, Hawkeye is preventing Gyges from doing what he ought to do.
4. One ought never to prevent someone from doing what he or she ought to do.
5. Therefore, Hawkeye ought not to prevent Gyges from escaping with the embezzled money.

Because premises 2 and 5 are contradictory, universal ethical egoism appears to be inconsistent.

The soundness of this argument depends, however, on premise 4, and defenders of universal ethical egoism believe there are grounds for rejecting this premise. For if "preventing an action" means "rendering the action impossible," it would appear that there *are* cases in which a person is justified in preventing someone else from doing what he or she ought to do. Suppose for example, that Irma and Igor are both actively competing for the same position at a prestigious law firm. If Irma accepts the position, she obviously renders it impossible for Igor to obtain the position. But surely this is *not* what we normally think of as an unacceptable form of prevention. Nor would Hawkeye's prevention of Gyges's escape appear to be unacceptable. Thus, to sustain the argument against universal ethical egoism, one must distinguish between acceptable and unacceptable forms of prevention and then show that the argument succeeds even for forms of prevention that a universal ethical egoist should regard as unacceptable. This requires elucidating the force of "ought" in universal ethical egoism.

To illustrate the sense in which a universal ethical egoist claims that other persons ought to do what is in their overall self-interest, defenders often appeal to an analogy of competitive games. For example, in football a defensive player might think that the opposing team's quarterback ought to pass on third down with five yards to go, while not wanting the quarterback to do so and planning to prevent any such attempt. Or to use Jesse Kalin's example:

> I may see how my chess opponent can put my king in check. This is how he ought to move. But believing that he ought to move his bishop and check my king does not commit me to wanting him to do that, nor to persuading him to do so. What I ought to do is sit there quietly, hoping he does not move as he ought.[10]

The point of these examples is to suggest that a universal ethical egoist may, like a player in a game, judge that others ought to do what is in their overall self-interest while simultaneously attempting to prevent such actions, or at least refraining from encouraging them.

The analogy of competitive games also illustrates the sense in which a universal ethical egoist claims that she herself ought to do what is in her overall self-interest. For just as a player's judgment that she ought to make a particular move is followed, other things being equal, by an attempt to perform the appropriate action, so likewise when a universal ethical egoist judges that she ought to do some particular action, other things being equal, an attempt to perform the appropriate action follows. In general, defenders of universal ethical egoism stress that because we have little difficulty understanding the implications of the use of "ought" in competitive games, we should also have little difficulty understanding the analogous use of "ought" by the universal ethical egoist.

To claim, however, that the "oughts" in competitive games are analogous to the "oughts" of universal ethical egoism does not mean there are no differences between them. Most importantly, competitive games are governed by moral constraints such that when everyone plays the game properly, there are acceptable moral limits as to what one can do. For example, in football one cannot poison the opposing quarterback in order to win the game. By contrast, when everyone holds self-interested reasons to be supreme, the only limit to what one can do is the point beyond which one ceases to benefit. But this important difference between the "oughts" of universal ethical egoism and the "oughts" found in publicly recognized activities like competitive games does not defeat the appropriateness of the analogy. That the "oughts" found in publicly recognized activities are always limited by various moral constraints (What else would get publicly recognized?) does not preclude their being a suggestive model for the unlimited action-guiding character of the "oughts" of universal ethical egoism.[11] What all this shows is that the most promising attempt to show that universal ethical egoism is inconsistent unfortunately fails to do so.

From Rationality to Morality

Yet despite our inability to show that universal ethical egoism is inconsistent, there are still grounds for showing that morality is rationally preferable to universal ethical egoism. This is because it can be shown that the universal ethical egoist, although consistent, acts contrary to reason in rejecting morality.[12]

To see this, let us imagine that each of us is capable of entertaining and acting upon both self-interested and moral reasons and that the question we are seeking to answer is what sort of reasons for action it would be rational for us to accept.[13] This question is not about what sort of reasons we should publicly affirm, since people will sometimes publicly affirm reasons that are quite different from those they are prepared to act upon. Rather it is a question about what reasons it would be rational for us to accept at the deepest level—in our heart of hearts.

Of course, there are people who are incapable of acting upon moral reasons. For such people, there is no question about their being required to act morally or altruistically. Yet the interesting philosophical question is not about such people but about people like ourselves, who are capable of acting morally as well as self-interestedly and are seeking a rational justification for following a particular course of action.

In trying to determine how we should act, let us assume that we would like to be able to construct a *good* argument favoring morality over egoism, and given that good arguments are non-question-begging, we accordingly would like to construct an argument that, as far as possible, does not beg the question. The question at issue here is what reasons each of us should take as supreme, and this question would be begged against egoism if we proposed to answer it simply by assuming from the start that moral reasons are the reasons that each of us should take as supreme. But the question would be begged against morality as well if we proposed to answer the question simply by assuming from the start that self-interested reasons are the reasons that each of us should take as supreme. This means, of course, that we cannot answer the question of what reasons we should take as supreme simply by assuming the general principle of egoism:

> Each person ought to do what best serves his or her overall self-interest.

We can no more argue for egoism simply by denying the relevance of moral reasons to rational choice than we can argue for pure altruism simply by denying the relevance of self-interested reasons to rational choice and assuming the following general principle of pure altruism:

> Each person ought to do what best serves the overall interest of others.[14]

Consequently, in order not to beg the question, we have no other alternative but to grant the prima facie relevance of both self-interested and moral reasons to rational choice and then try to determine which reasons we would be rationally required to act upon, all things considered. Notice that in order not to beg the question, it is necessary to back off from both the general principle of egoism and the general principle of pure altruism, thus granting the prima facie relevance of both self-interested and moral reasons to rational choice. From this standpoint, it is still an open question whether either egoism or pure altruism will be rationally preferable, all things considered.

In this regard, there are two kinds of cases that must be considered: cases in which there is a conflict between the relevant self-interested and moral reasons, and cases in which there is no such conflict.

It seems obvious that where there is no conflict and both reasons are conclusive reasons of their kind, both reasons should be acted upon. In such contexts, we should do what is favored both by morality and by self-interest.

Consider the following example. Suppose you accepted a job marketing a baby formula in a developing country where the formula was improperly used, leading to increased infant mortality.[15] Imagine that you could just as well have accepted an equally attractive and rewarding job marketing a similar formula in a developed country, where the misuse does not occur, so that a rational weighing of the relevant self-interested reasons alone would not have favored your acceptance of one of these jobs over the other.[16] At the same time, there were obviously moral reasons that condemned your acceptance of the first job—reasons that you presumably are or were able to acquire. Moreover, by assumption in this case, the moral reasons do not clash with the relevant self-interested reasons; they simply made a recommendation where the relevant self-interested reasons were silent. Consequently, a rational weighing of all the relevant reasons in this case could not but favor acting in accord with the relevant moral reasons.[17]

Yet it might be objected that in cases of this sort there would frequently be other reasons significantly opposed to these moral reasons—other reasons that you are or were able to acquire. Such reasons would be either *malevolent*, seeking to bring about the suffering and death of other human beings; *benevolent*, concerned to promote nonhuman welfare even at the expense of human welfare; or *aesthetic*, concerned to produce valuable results irrespective of the effects on human or nonhuman welfare. But assuming that such malevolent reasons are ultimately rooted in some conception of what is good for oneself or others,[18] these reasons would have already been taken into account, and by assumption outweighed by the other relevant reasons in this case. And although neither benevolent reasons (concerned to promote nonhuman welfare) nor aesthetic reasons would have been taken into account, such reasons are not directly relevant to justifying morality over egoism.[19] Consequently, even with the presence of these three kinds of reasons, your acceptance of the first job can still be seen to be contrary to the relevant reasons in this case.

Needless to say, defenders of egoism cannot but be disconcerted with this result since it shows that actions in accord with egoism are contrary to reason at least when there are two equally good ways of pursuing one's self-interest, only one of which does not conflict with the basic requirements of morality. Notice also that in cases where there are two equally good ways of fulfilling the basic requirements of morality, only one of which does not conflict with what is in a person's overall self-interest, it is not at all disconcerting for defenders of morality to admit that we are rationally required to choose the way that does not conflict with what is in our overall self-interest. Nevertheless, exposing this defect in egoism for cases where moral reasons and self-interested reasons do not conflict would be but a small victory for defenders of morality if it were not also possible to show that in cases where such reasons do conflict, moral reasons would have priority over self-interested reasons.

Now when we rationally assess the relevant reasons in conflict cases, it is best to cast the conflict not as a conflict between self-interested reasons and moral reasons but instead as a conflict between self-interested reasons and altruistic reasons.[20] Viewed in this way, three solutions are possible. First, we could say that self-interested reasons always have priority over conflicting altruistic reasons. Second, we could say just the opposite, that altruistic reasons always have priority over conflicting self-interested reasons. Third, we could say that some kind of compromise is rationally required. In this compromise, sometimes self-interested reasons would have priority over altruistic reasons, and sometimes altruistic reasons would have priority over self-interested reasons.

Once the conflict is described in this manner, the third solution can be seen to be the one that is rationally required. This is because the first and second solutions give exclusive priority to one class of relevant reasons over the other, and only a completely question-begging justification can be given for such an exclusive priority. Only by employing the third solution, and sometimes giving priority to self-interested reasons, and sometimes giving priority to altruistic reasons, can we avoid a completely question-begging resolution.

Suppose for example, that you are in the waste disposal business and you have decided to dispose of toxic wastes in a manner that is cost-efficient for you but predictably causes significant harm to future generations. Imagine that there are alternative methods available for disposing of the waste that are only slightly less cost-efficient and will not cause any significant harm to future generations.[21] In this case, you are to weigh your self-interested reasons favoring the most cost-efficient disposal of the toxic wastes against the relevant altruistic reasons favoring the avoidance of significant harm to future generations. If we suppose that the projected loss of benefit to yourself was ever so slight and the projected harm to future generations was ever so great, then a nonarbitrary compromise between the relevant self-interested and altruistic reasons would have to favor the altruistic reasons in this case. Hence, as judged by a non-question-begging standard of rationality, your method of waste disposal was contrary to the relevant reasons.

Notice also that this standard of rationality will not support just any compromise between the relevant self-interested and altruistic reasons. The compromise must be a nonarbitrary one, for otherwise it would beg the question with respect to the opposing egoistic and altruistic perspectives.[22] Such a compromise would have to respect the rankings of self-interested and altruistic reasons imposed by the egoistic and altruistic perspectives, respectively. Since for each individual there is a separate ranking of that individual's relevant self-interested and altruistic reasons (which will vary, of course, depending on the individual's capabilities and circumstances), we can represent these rankings from the most important reasons to the least important reasons as follows:

Individual A		Individual B	
Self-interested Reasons	Altruistic Reasons	Self-interested Reasons	Altruistic Reasons
1	1	1	1
2	2	2	2
3	3	3	3
•	•	•	•
•	•	•	•
•	•	•	•
N	N	N	N

Accordingly, any nonarbitrary compromise among such reasons in seeking not to beg the question against either egoism or pure altruism will have to give priority to those reasons that rank highest in each category. Failure to give priority to the highest-ranking altruistic or self-interested reasons would, other things being equal, be contrary to reason.

Of course, there will be cases in which the only way to avoid being required to do what is contrary to your highest-ranking reasons is by requiring someone else to do what is contrary to her highest-ranking reasons. Some of these cases will be "lifeboat cases," as, for example, where you and two others are stranded on a lifeboat that has only enough resources for two of you to survive before you will be rescued. But although such cases are surely difficult to resolve (maybe only a chance mechanism, like flipping a coin, can offer a reasonable resolution), they surely do not reflect the typical conflict between the relevant self-interested and altruistic reasons that we are or were able to acquire. Typically, one or the other of the conflicting reasons will rank significantly higher on its respective scale, thus permitting a clear resolution.

Now we can see how morality can be viewed as just such a nonarbitrary compromise between self-interested and altruistic reasons. First, a certain amount of self-regard is morally required or at least morally acceptable. Where this is the case, high-ranking self-interested reasons have priority over low-ranking altruistic reasons. Second, morality obviously places limits on the extent to which people should pursue their own self-interest. Where this is the case, high-ranking altruistic reasons have priority over low-ranking self-interested reasons. In this way, morality can be seen to be a nonarbitrary compromise between self-interested and altruistic reasons, and the "moral reasons" that constitute that compromise can be seen as having an absolute priority over the self-interested or altruistic reasons that conflict with them.[23]

It is also important to see how this compromise view has been supported by a two-step argument that is not question-begging at all. In the first step, our goal was to determine what sort of reasons for action it would be rational for us to accept on the basis of a good argument, and this required a non-question-begging starting point. Noting that both egoism, which favored exclusively self-interested reasons, and pure altruism, which favored exclusively altruistic reasons, offered only question-begging starting points, we took as our non-question-begging starting point the prima facie relevance of both self-interested and altruistic reasons to rational choice. The logical inference here is analogous to the inference of equal probability sanctioned in decision theory when we have no evidence that one alternative is more likely than another.[24] Here we had no non-question-begging justification for excluding either self-interested or altruistic reasons as relevant to rational choice, so we accepted both kinds of reasons as prima facie relevant to rational choice. The conclusion of this first step of the argument for the compromise view does not beg the question against egoism or pure altruism because if defenders of either view had any hope of providing a good and, hence, non-question-begging argument for their views, they too would have to grant this very conclusion as necessary for a non-question-begging defense of either egoism, pure altruism, or the compromise view. In accepting it, therefore, the compromise view does not beg the question against a possible non-question-begging defense of these other two perspectives, and that is all that should concern us.

Now once both self-interested and altruistic reasons are recognized as prima facie relevant to rational choice, the second step of the argument for the compromise view offers a nonarbitrary ordering of those reasons on the basis of rankings of self-interested and altruistic reasons imposed by the egoistic and altruistic perspectives respectively. According to that ordering, high-ranking self-interested reasons have priority over low-ranking altruistic reasons and high-ranking altruistic reasons have priority over low-ranking self-interested reasons. There is no other plausible nonarbitrary ordering of these reasons. Hence, it certainly does not beg the question against either the egoistic or altruistic perspective, once we imagine those perspectives (or their defenders) to be suitably reformed so that they too are committed to a standard of non-question-beggingness. In the end, if one is committed to a standard of non-question-beggingness, one has to be concerned only with how one's claims and arguments stack up against others who are also committed to such a standard. If you yourself are committed to the standard of non-question-beggingness, you don't beg the question by simply coming into conflict with the requirements of other perspectives, unless those other perspectives (or their defenders) are also committed to the same standard of non-question-beggingness. In arguing for one's view, when one comes into conflict with bigots, one does not beg the question against them unless one is a bigot oneself.

Suppose, for example, that we are trying to decide who are the two greatest moral and political philosophers of the twentieth century. Suppose some of us assume from the start that the two must belong to the British-American tradition and proceed to nominate John Rawls and R. M. Hare, while the others assume from the start that the two must belong to the Continental tradition and nominate Jurgen Habermas and Jean-Paul Sartre.[25] By contrast, a compromise view, in order not to beg the question, would start by assuming that the two greatest moral and political philosophers of the twentieth century could belong to either the British-American or the Continental tradition or, for that matter, to any philosophical tradition, and it might well proceed to nominate John Rawls and Jurgen Habermas. This would put the compromise view partly in conflict and partly in agreement with the two other views taken in this discussion, but it would not show that it begged the question against them, because they did not approach the discussion in a non-question-begging manner. Again, being in conflict with bigots does not necessarily make one a bigot; to be a bigot, you yourself must also be arguing from a question-begging standpoint.

Accordingly, it would be a mistake to think that the conflicts that exist between the compromise view and either an unreformed egoistic or an unreformed altruistic perspective is grounds for thinking that the compromise view begs the question against those perspectives. Thus, we can imagine an unreformed altruistic perspective as holding that:

(1) All high-ranking altruistic reasons have priority over conflicting lower-ranking self-interested reasons.
(2) All low-ranking altruistic reasons have priority over conflicting higher-ranking self-interested reasons.

And we can also imagine an unreformed egoistic perspective as holding that:

(1′) All high-ranking self-interested reasons have priority over conflicting lower-ranking altruistic reasons.
(2′) All low-ranking self-interested reasons have priority over conflicting higher-ranking altruistic reasons.[26]

By contrast, the compromise view holds (1) and (1′). Now one might think that part of what the compromise view holds about the priority of reasons—i.e., (1)—begs the question against an unreformed egoistic perspective, and another part—i.e., (1′)—begs the question against an unreformed altruistic perspective; hence, to that extent, one might conclude that the compromise view does beg the question against each view.[27] But there is no reason to view the conflicts between the compromise view and an unreformed egoistic perspective or an unreformed altruistic perspective as begging the question against those perspectives. To beg the question, it is not enough that one is in complete or partial conflict with someone else's view; you, or both you and they, must also be proceeding from a question-begging standpoint. And this is clearly not the case with respect to the compromise view.

Now it might be objected that even if morality is required by a standard of non-question-beggingness, that does not provide us with the right kind of reason to be moral. It might be argued that avoiding non-question-beggingness is too formal a reason to be moral and that we need a more substantive reason.[28] Happily, the need for a substantive reason to be moral can be met, because in this case the formal reason to be moral—namely, avoiding non-question-beggingness—itself entails a substantive reason to be moral—namely, to give high-ranking altruistic reasons priority over conflicting lower-ranking self-interested reasons and high-ranking self-interested reasons priority over conflicting lower-ranking altruistic reasons, or, to put the reason more substantively still, to avoid inflicting basic harm for the sake of nonbasic benefit. So, as it turns out, morality as compromise can be shown to provide both formal and substantive reasons to be moral.

Of course, exactly how this compromise is to be worked out is a matter of considerable debate, which brings us to our third problem of traditional ethics—the problem of practical requirements. Yet however this debate over practical requirements is resolved, it is clear that some sort of compromise moral solution is rationally preferable to either egoism or pure altruism when judged from a non-question-begging standpoint.[29]

The Problem of Practical Requirements: What Does Morality Require?

Obviously, there are various ways to interpret morality as a compromise between self-interested and altruistic reasons to determine what morality requires. The best-known interpretations are those of utilitarian ethics, Aristotelian ethics, and Kantian ethics.[30] The basic principle of a utilitarian ethics is:

> Do those actions that would maximize the net utility or satisfaction of everyone affected by them.

A utilitarian ethics can be understood as a compromise between self-interested and altruistic reasons, because it takes the utility or satisfaction of all those affected equally into account.

To illustrate, let's consider how this ethics applies to the question of whether nation A should intervene in the internal affairs of

nation B when nation A's choice would have the following consequences:

	Nation A's Choice	
	Intervene	**Don't Intervene**
Net utility to A	4 trillion units	8.5 trillion units
Net utility to B	2 trillion units	−2 trillion units
Total utility	6 trillion units	6.5 trillion units

Given that these are all the consequences that are relevant to nation A's choice, a utilitarian ethics favors not intervening. Note
that in this case, the choice favoring a utilitarian ethics does not
conflict with the group interest of nation A, although it does conflict with the group interest of nation B.

But are such calculations of utility possible? Admittedly, they
are difficult to make. At the same time, such calculations seem to
serve as a basis for public discussion. Once, President Reagan, addressing a group of African-American business leaders, asked
whether African Americans were better off because of the Great
Society programs, and although many disagreed with the answer
he gave, no one found his question unanswerable.[31] Thus, faced
with the exigencies of measuring utility, a utilitarian ethics simply counsels that we do our best to determine what would maximize net utility and act on the result.

The second ethics to be considered is an Aristotelian ethics. Its
basic principle is:

> Do those actions that would further one's proper development
> as a human being.

This ethics can also be understood as a compromise between self-interested and altruistic reasons, because what furthers one's proper development as a human being, according to this view, clearly involves
taking both self-interested and altruistic reasons into account.

There are, however, different versions of this ethics. According
to some versions, each person can determine through the use of reason his or her proper development as a human being. Other ver-

sions disagree. For example, many religious traditions rely on revelation to guide people in their proper development as human beings. However, although an Aristotelian ethics can take these various forms, I want to focus on what is probably its philosophically most interesting form.[32] That form specifies proper development in terms of virtuous activity and understands virtuous activity to preclude intentionally doing evil whatever the consequences. In this form, an Aristotelian ethics conflicts most radically with a utilitarian ethics, which specifies virtuous activity solely in terms of the consequences for the satisfaction or utility of everyone affected.

The third ethics to be considered is a Kantian ethics. This ethics has its origins in seventeenth- and eighteenth-century social contract theories, which tended to rely on actual contracts to specify moral requirements. However, actual contracts may or may not have been made, and, even if they were made, they may or may not have been moral or fair. This led Immanuel Kant and contemporary Kantian John Rawls to resort to hypothetical contracts to ground moral requirements. A difficulty with this ethics is in determining under what conditions a hypothetical contract is fair and moral. Currently, the most favored Kantian ethics is specified by the following basic principle:

> Do those actions that persons behind an imaginary veil of ignorance would unanimously agree should be done.[33]

This imaginary veil extends to most particular facts about oneself—anything that would bias one's choice or stand in the way of a unanimous agreement. Accordingly, the imaginary veil of ignorance would mask one's knowledge of one's social position, talents, sex, race, and religion, but not one's knowledge of such general information as would be contained in political, social, economic, and psychological theories. This Kantian ethics can also be understood as a compromise between self-interested and altruistic reasons because its imaginary veil of ignorance takes both self and others appropriately into account.

To illustrate this ethics, let's return to the example of nation A and nation B used earlier. The choice facing nation A was the following:

	Nation A's Choice	
	Intervene	**Don't Intervene**
Net utility to A	4 trillion units	8.5 trillion units
Net utility to B	2 trillion units	−2 trillion units
Total utility	6 trillion units	6.5 trillion units

Given that these are all the consequences relevant to nation A's choice, a Kantian ethics favors intervention because persons behind the imaginary veil of ignorance would have to consider that they might turn out to be in nation B, and in that case, they would not want to be so disadvantaged for the greater benefit of those in nation A. This resolution conflicts with the resolution favored by a utilitarian ethics and the group interest of nation A, but not with the group interest of nation B.

Assessing Alternative Ethics

Needless to say, each of these interpretations of morality has its strengths and weaknesses. The main strength of a utilitarian ethics is that once the relevant utilities are determined, there is an effective decision-making procedure that can be used to resolve all practical problems. After determining the relevant utilities, all that remains is to total the net utilities and choose the alternative with the highest net utility. The basic weakness of this interpretation of morality, however, is that it does not give sufficient weight to the distribution of utility among the relevant parties. For example, consider a society equally divided between the privileged rich and the alienated poor, which faces the following alternatives:

	Nation A's Choice	
	Alternative A	**Alternative B**
Net utility to privileged rich	5.5 trillion units	4 trillion units
Net utility to alienated poor	1 trillion units	2 trillion units
Total utility	6.5 trillion units	6 trillion units

Given that these are all the relevant utilities, a utilitarian ethics favors alternative A even though alternative B provides a higher minimum payoff. And if the utility values for two alternatives were:

	Nation A's Choice	
	Alternative A	**Alternative B**
Net utility to privileged rich	4 trillion units	5 trillion units
Net utility to alienated poor	2 trillion units	1 trillion units
Total utility	6 trillion units	6 trillion units

a utilitarian ethics would be indifferent between the alternatives, despite the fact that alternative A again provides a higher minimum payoff. In this way, a utilitarian ethics fails to take into account the distribution of utility among the relevant parties. All that matters for this ethics is maximizing total utility, and the distribution of utility among the affected parties is taken into account only insofar as it contributes toward the attainment of that goal.

By contrast, the main strength of an Aristotelian ethics in the form we are considering is that it restricts the means that can be chosen in pursuit of good consequences. In particular, it absolutely prohibits intentionally doing evil whatever the consequences. However, although some restriction on the means available for the pursuit of good consequences seems desirable, the main weakness of this version of an Aristotelian ethics is that the restriction it imposes is too strong. Indeed, exceptions to this restriction would seem to be justified whenever the evil to be done is:

1. Trivial (e.g., stepping on someone's foot to get out of a crowded subway).
2. Easily reparable (e.g., lying to a temporarily depressed friend to keep her from committing suicide).
3. Sufficiently outweighed by the consequences of the action (e.g., shooting one of two hundred civilian hostages to prevent in the only way possible the execution of all two hundred).

Still another weakness of this ethics is that it lacks an effective decision-making procedure for resolving practical problems. Beyond imposing a restriction on the means that can be employed in the pursuit of good consequences, the advocates of this ethics have not agreed on criteria for selecting among the available alternatives.

The main strength of a Kantian ethics is that, like an Aristotelian ethics, it seeks to restrict the means available for the pursuit of good consequences. However, unlike the version of an Aristotelian ethics we considered, a Kantian ethics does not impose an absolute restriction on intentionally doing evil. Behind the veil of ignorance, persons would surely agree that if the evil were trivial, easily reparable, or sufficiently outweighed by the consequences, there would be an adequate justification for permitting it. On the other hand, it would appear that the main weakness of a Kantian ethics is that although it provides an effective decision-making procedure for resolving some practical problems, such as the problem of how to distribute income and wealth and the problem of distant peoples and future generations, it will not work for the problems of animal rights and environmental justice. For how are we to imagine animals and plants choosing behind the veil of ignorance?

But while it may be difficult, if not impossible, to imagine ourselves being animals and plants, it does seem possible to formulate a Kantian ethics more generally so as to allow for the possibility that the interests of nonhumans could count. So formulated, the basic principle of a Kantian ethics would be:

> Do those actions that would be unanimously agreed to behind a veil of ignorance from the standpoint of all those affected by them.

Given this formulation, actions would be unanimously agreed to behind a veil of ignorance from the standpoint of nonhumans if *human* advocates of the interests of nonhumans, acting reasonably, would also agree to such actions, just as actions would be unanimously agreed to behind a veil of ignorance from the standpoint of nonrational humans if human advocates of the interests of nonrational humans, acting reasonably, would also agree to such actions.

Yet while it is possible to formulate a Kantian ethics in a way that allows for the possibility that the interests of nonhumans count, this has not generally been done. In fact, advocates of traditional ethics have generally failed to take into account the interests of nonhuman living beings, which, of course, is what has occasioned the challenge of environmentalism. Nevertheless, traditional ethics is not without resources for dealing with this challenge as well as the challenges of feminism and multiculturalism. That is what consideration of the problems of relativism (Is morality relative?), rationality (Is morality rationally required?), and practical requirements (What does morality require?) in this chapter sought to establish. Thus, if I am right, traditional ethics is capable of showing that:

(1) Moral relativism is an implausible theory.
(2) Morality is rationally required and not just rationally permissible.
(3) There are good reasons for favoring the requirements of a Kantian ethics as I have formulated it.

Accordingly, given these and other accomplishments of traditional ethics, it should not be that difficult for us to go on to address the challenges of environmentalism, feminism, and multiculturalism and give them their due.

2

ENVIRONMENTALISM

The Human Bias in Traditional Ethics and How to Correct It

The failure of traditional ethics to sufficiently take into account the interests of nonhuman living beings is what gives rise to the challenge of environmentalism that traditional ethics is biased in favor of humans. Recent interest in this challenge to traditional ethics dates from the publication of Peter Singer's article "Animal Liberation" in the *New York Review of Books* in 1973, followed by the publication two years later of his book of the same title.[1] Singer focused attention on two of the most serious forms of animal exploitation: factory farming and animal experimentation.

In factory farming, millions of animals are raised in such a way that their short lives are dominated by pain and suffering. Veal calves are put in narrow stalls and tethered with a chain so that they cannot turn around, lie down comfortably, or groom themselves. They are fed a totally liquid diet deprived of iron to promote rapid weight gain and to maintain anemia, and they are given no water because thirsty animals eat more than those who drink water. Animal experimentation is also a big business, involving about 200 million animals a year worldwide.[2] A large percentage of these animals are used in commercial toxicity tests such as the rabbit-blinding Draize eye test and the widely used and widely criticized LD50 toxicity test designed to find the lethal dose for 50 percent of a sample of animals.

Singer's Utilitarian Environmentalism

Singer argues for the liberation of animals by comparing the bias against animals, which he calls "speciesism," with biases against blacks and women. According to Singer, the grounds we have for opposing racism and sexism are also grounds for opposing speciesism, because all forms of discrimination run counter to the principle of equal consideration, which is a central principle of a utilitarian ethics. According to Singer, racists violate this principle by unjustifiably giving greater weight to the interests of members of their own race in cases of conflict; sexists violate this principle by unjustifiably giving greater weight to the interests of members of their own sex in cases of conflict; and speciesists violate this principle by unjustifiably giving greater weight to the interests of members of their own species in cases of conflict.

Animals have interests, Singer maintains, because they have a capacity for suffering and enjoyment. According to the principle of equal consideration, there is no justification for regarding the pain animals feel as less important than the same amount of pain (or pleasure) humans feel. As for the practical requirements of this view, Singer contends that we cannot go astray if we give the same respect to the lives of animals that we give to the lives of humans at a similar mental level. In the end, Singer thinks, this will require us to make radical changes in our diet, the farming methods we use, experimental procedures in many fields of science, our approach to wildlife and to hunting, trapping and the wearing of furs, and areas of entertainment like circuses, rodeos, and zoos.

Regan's Kantian Environmentalism

Around the same time that Singer was developing his utilitarian environmentalism on behalf of animal liberation, Tom Regan was proposing a Kantian environmentalism.[3] According to Regan, what is fundamentally wrong with our treatment of nonhuman animals is that it implies that they are simply resources for our use. Regan argues that the correct grounding for our duties to animals and their rights against us is their inherent value, which they possess equally with ourselves, as experiencing subjects of life. Because animals, who are experiencing subjects of life, are entitled to equal respect, Regan argues that we should totally abolish the use of animals in science, end commercial animal agriculture, and eliminate both commercial and sport hunting and trapping. To those who might concede that animals have inherent value but to a lesser degree than humans, Regan argues that this view would only be defensible if similarly deficient humans were also seen as having less inherent value—a stance Regan feels his opponents are not willing to take.

A serious problem with both Singer's and Regan's views, however, is that they both still appear to be biased against certain forms of life. In the case of Singer's view, it is not clear why only *sentient* beings count and not all living beings. Singer maintains that only sentient beings have interests in the sense that what we do matters to them, but why should this be grounds for excluding non-sentient living beings from moral consideration, given that although they are nonsentient, they still have a good of their own? In the case of Regan's view, it is not clear why only *experiencing* subjects of life have inherent value and not all subjects of life. Regan recognizes that nonexperiencing subjects of life have a good of their own, but he does not explain why this does not suffice for them to count morally. This particular challenge to both Singer's and Regan's views is taken up by Paul Taylor. Taylor defends an alternative Kantian environmentalism that morally takes into account the interests of all individual living beings.

Taylor's Kantian Environmentalism

According to Taylor, all individual living beings can be benefited or harmed and have a good of their own, and, hence, qualify as moral subjects.[4] However, Taylor denies that species themselves are moral subjects with a good of their own, because he regards "species" as a class name, and classes, he contends, have no good of their own.[5] Therefore, his view has been called "biocentric individualism."

Yet species are unlike abstract classes in that they evolve, split, bud off new species, become endangered, go extinct, and have interests distinct from the interests of their members.[6] For example, a particular species of deer, but not individual members of that species, can have an interest in being preyed upon. Hence, species can be benefited and harmed and have a good of their own, and so should qualify in Taylor's view as moral subjects. So too, in Taylor's view, ecosystems should qualify as moral subjects since they can be benefited and harmed and have a good of their own, having features and interests not shared by their components.[7] To signal this modification in Taylor's environmentalism so that it also recognizes that species and ecosystems can be moral subjects with goods of their own, we can rename the modified view "biocentric pluralism."

According to Taylor, however, showing that entities have a good of their own does not establish that we ought to respect them.[8] To establish that, Taylor claims it is necessary to establish the following four theses:

(1) Humans are members of the earth's community of life.
(2) All living things are related to one another in an order of interdependence.
(3) Each organism is a teleological center of life.
(4) The assertion of human superiority is groundless.[9]

Taylor spends most of his time arguing for thesis 4 since the other three theses are difficult to reject.[10] To establish 4, Taylor argues that we have no non-question-begging grounds for regarding the members of any living species as superior to the members of any other. He allows that the members of species differ in myriad ways, but argues that these differences do not provide grounds for thinking that the members of any one species are superior to the members of any other. In particular, Taylor denies that the differences between species provide grounds for thinking that humans are superior to the members of other species. Taylor recognizes that humans have distinctive traits which the members of other species lack, such as rationality and moral agency. He just points out that the members of nonhuman species also have distinctive traits that humans lack, such as the homing ability of pigeons, the speed of cheetahs, and the ruminative ability of sheep and cattle.

Nor will it do to claim that the distinctive traits that humans have are more valuable than the distinctive traits that members of other species possess, because there is no non-question-begging standpoint from which to justify that claim. From a human standpoint, rationality and moral agency are more valuable than any of the distinctive traits found in nonhuman species, since, as humans, we would not be better off if we were to trade in those traits for the distinctive traits found in nonhuman species. Yet the same holds true of nonhuman species. Generally pigeons, cheetahs, sheep and cattle would not be better off if they were to trade in their distinctive traits for the distinctive traits of other species.

Of course, the members of some species might be better off if they could retain the distinctive traits of their species while acquiring one or another of the distinctive traits possessed by some other species. For example, we humans might be better off if we could retain our distinctive traits while acquiring the ruminative ability of sheep and cattle.[11] But many of the distinctive traits of species cannot be even imaginatively added to the members of other species without substantially altering the original species. For example, in order for the cheetah to acquire the distinctive traits possessed by humans, presumably it would have to be so transformed that its paws became something like hands to accommodate its humanlike mental capabilities, thereby losing its distinctive speed and ceasing to be a cheetah. So possessing distinctively human traits would not be good for the cheetah.[12] And with the possible exception of our nearest evolutionary relatives, the same holds true for the members of other species: they would not be better off having distinctively human traits.[13] Only in fairy tales and in the world of Disney can the members of nonhuman species enjoy a full array of distinctively human traits. So there would appear to be no non-question-begging perspective from which to judge that distinctively human traits are more valuable than the distinctive traits possessed by other species. Judged from a non-question-begging perspective, Taylor contends, the assertion of human superiority is groundless.

According to Taylor, given the groundlessness of the assertion of the claim to human superiority and the support that can be given for the first three theses of the biocentric outlook, the claim to human superiority must be rejected by any rational and informed person.[14] Taylor further argues that the rejection of this claim to human superiority and, more generally, of the claim that any species is inherently superior to any other, entails as its positive counterpart a principle of species impartiality.[15]

Nevertheless, it is possible to recast Taylor's argument here so that it rests more directly on normative premises.[16] Consider the following formulation:

(1) We should not aggress against any living being unless there are either self-evident or non-question-begging reasons for doing so. (It would be difficult to reject this principle given the various analogous principles we accept, such as the principle of formal equality: equals should be treated equally and unequals unequally.)

(2) To treat humans as superior overall to other living beings is to aggress against them by sacrificing their basic needs to meet the nonbasic needs of humans. (definition)

(3) Therefore, we should not treat humans as superior overall to other living beings unless we have either self-evident or non-question-begging reasons for doing so. (from 1 and 2)

(4) We do not have either self-evident or non-question-begging reasons for treating humans as superior overall to other living beings. (That we do not have any non-question-begging reasons for treating humans as superior overall to other living beings was established by the previous argument.[17] That we do not have any self-evident reasons for doing so, I take it, is obvious.)

(5) Therefore, we should not treat humans as superior overall to other living beings. (from 3 and 4)

(6) Not to treat humans as superior overall to other living beings is to treat them as equal overall to other living beings.[18] (definition)

(7) Therefore, we should treat humans as equal overall to other living beings. (from 5 and 6)

As I indicated, the advantage of this formulation of the argument for biocentric pluralism is that it clearly indicates the normative premises on which the argument rests (1 and to a lesser degree 4). In Taylor's formulation, one is never quite sure how the argument proceeds. Taylor is so concerned to establish that he is not making any illicit move from facts to values or from "is" to "ought" that he never clearly indicates the complete set of oughts or values from which his principle of species-impartiality is to be derived.[19] Biocentric pluralism remedies this defect in Taylor's environmentalism.

Priority Principles for Biocentric Pluralism

In order to make clear what are the practical implications of his theory, Taylor sets out a number of priority principles.[20] As it turns out, these principles need to be modified and defended in order to establish what are the practical implications of biocentric pluralism.

Taylor's first priority principle is the following:

> *A Principle of Self-Defense*
> Actions are permissible that are absolutely required for maintaining the very existence of moral agents and enabling them to exercise the capacity for moral agency.[21]

However, the content of this principle is better understood, I think, if it is split into two principles. The first is:

> *A Principle of Human Defense*
> Actions that defend oneself and other human beings against harmful aggression are permissible even when they necessitate killing or harming individual animals or plants or even destroying whole species or ecosystems.[22]

This Principle of Human Defense allows us to defend ourselves and other human beings from harmful aggression (1) against our persons and the persons of other human beings that we are committed to or happen to care about, and (2) against our justifiably held property and the justifiably held property of other human beings that we are committed to or happen to care about.[23]

This principle is analogous to the principle of self-defense that applies in traditional ethics and permits actions in defense of oneself or other human beings against harmful human aggression.[24] In the case of human aggression, however, it will sometimes be possible to effectively defend oneself and other human beings by first suffering the aggression and then securing adequate compensation later. Since in cases of nonhuman aggression, this is unlikely to obtain, more harmful preventive actions such as killing a rabid dog or swatting a mosquito will be justified. There are simply more effective ways stop aggressive humans than there are to stop aggressive nonhumans.[25]

The other principle we need to replace Taylor's principle is:

> *A Principle of Human Preservation*
> Actions that are necessary for meeting one's basic needs or the basic needs of other human beings are permissible even when they require aggressing against the basic needs of individual animals and plants or even of whole species or ecosystems.[26]

Now needs, in general, if not satisfied, lead to lacks or deficiencies with respect to various standards. The basic needs of humans, if not satisfied, lead to lacks or deficiencies with respect to a standard of a decent life. The basic needs of animals and plants, if not satisfied, lead to lacks or deficiencies with respect to a standard of a healthy life. The basic needs of species and ecosystems, if not satisfied, lead to lacks or deficiencies with respect to a standard of a healthy living system. The means necessary for meeting the basic needs of humans can vary widely from society to society. By contrast, the means necessary for meeting the basic needs of particular species of animals and plants tend to be invariant.[27] Of course, while only some needs can be clearly classified as basic, and others clearly classified as nonbasic, there still are other needs that are more or less difficult to classify. Yet the fact that not every need can be clearly classified as either basic or nonbasic, as is true of a whole range of dichotomous concepts like moral/immoral, legal/illegal, living/nonliving, human/nonhuman, should not immobilize us from acting at least with respect to clear cases.

In traditional ethics, there is no principle that is strictly analogous to this Principle of Human Preservation.[28] There is a principle of self-preservation in traditional ethics that permits actions that are necessary for meeting one's own basic needs or the basic needs of other people, even if this requires *failing to meet* (through an act of omission) the basic needs of still other people. For example, we can use our resources to feed ourselves and our family, even if this necessitates failing to meet the basic needs of people in developing countries. But, in general, we don't have a principle that allows us to *aggress against* (through an act of commission) the basic needs of some people in order to meet our own basic needs or the basic needs of other people to whom we are committed or happen to care about. Actually, the closest we come to permitting aggressing against the basic needs of other people in order to meet our own basic needs or the basic needs of people to whom we are committed or happen to care about is our acceptance of the outcome of life-and-death struggles in lifeboat cases, where no one has an antecedent right to the available resources. For example, if you had to fight off others in order to secure the last place in a lifeboat for yourself or for a member of your family, we might say that you justifiably aggressed against the basic needs of those whom you fought to meet your own basic needs or the basic needs of the member of your family.[29]

Now the Principle of Human Preservation does not permit aggressing against the basic needs of humans even if it is the only way to meet our own basic needs or the basic needs of other human beings. Rather this principle is directed at a different range of cases with respect to which we can meet our own basic needs and the basic needs of other humans simply by aggressing against the basic needs of nonhuman living beings. With respect to these cases, the Principle of Human Preservation permits actions that are necessary for meeting one's own basic needs or the basic needs of other human beings even when they require aggressing against the basic needs of individual animals and plants or even of whole species or ecosystems.

Of course, we could envision an even more permissive principle of human perservation, one that would permit us to aggress against the basic needs of both humans and nonhumans to meet our own basic needs or the basic needs of other human beings. But while adopting such a principle, by permitting cannibalism, would clearly reduce the degree of predation of humans on other species, and so would be of some benefit to other species, it would clearly be counterproductive with respect to meeting basic human needs. This is because implicit nonaggression pacts based on a reasonable expectation of a comparable degree of altruistic forebearance from fellow humans have been enormously beneficial and probably were necessary for the survival of the human species. So it is difficult to see how it would be in the interest of humans to forgo such benefits when they can easily meet their basic needs by simply aggressing against the basic needs of the members of nonhuman species. In this case, the moral permissibility of meeting basic human needs in this way would remain.

Of course, we may be required to meet our basic needs by aggressing against the basic needs of the members of some nonhuman species rather than others, for example, in order to protect endangered species. But while some such qualifications may be morally required, they will not undermine the general moral acceptability of the Principle of Human Preservation.[30] Accordingly, the Principles of Human Defense and Human Preservation, with their accompanying justification, make clear what is, at best, implicit in Taylor's Principle of Defense.

Taylor's next two principles are:

A Principle of Proportionality
Actions that pursue nonbasic human interests are prohibited when they aggress against the basic interests of (wild) animals and plants, and are incompatible with the attitude of respect for nature.

A Principle of Minimal Harm
Actions that pursue certain nonbasic human interests are permissible even when they aggress against the basic interests of (wild) animals and plants provided that they are compatible with the attitude of respect for nature and provided that no alternative way of pursuing those nonbasic human interests would involve fewer wrongs.[31]

However, what it is difficult to comprehend is how, according to these principles, some ways of aggressing against the basic needs of (wild) animals and plants are incompatible with the attitude of respect for nature whereas other ways of aggressing against the basic needs of (wild) animals and plants are compatible with the attitude of respect for nature. These principles just seem inconsistent with the rest of Taylor's theory.

As examples of actions that are prohibited by the Principle of Proportionality, Taylor cites the slaughtering of elephants so the ivory of their tusks can be used to carve items for the tourist trade and all hunting and fishing which is done as an enjoyable pastime.[32] As examples of actions that are permitted by the Principle of Minimal Harm, he cites building a library where natural habitat must be destroyed and constructing an airport, railroad, harbor or highway involving the serious disturbance of a natural ecosystem.[33] Given these examples, it would be preferable to consider the actions that Taylor regards as permitted by the Principle of Minimal Harm as serving basic rather than nonbasic human needs, or at least as justified when they do serve such needs.[34] If we do this, we can replace these two principles with just one. It is:

> A Principle of Disproportionality
> Actions that meet nonbasic or luxury needs of humans are prohibited when they aggress against the basic needs of individual animals and plants, or of whole species or ecosystems.

Now this principle is strictly analogous to a principle found in traditional ethics that prohibits meeting some people's nonbasic or luxury needs when it conflicts with satisfying the basic needs of other people.[35]

Without a doubt, the adoption of such a principle with respect to nonhuman nature would significantly change the way we live our lives. Such a principle is required, however, if there is to be any substance to the claim that all living beings are equal. We can no more consistently claim that all living beings are equal and yet aggress against the basic needs of some living beings whenever this serves our own nonbasic or luxury needs than we can consistently claim that all humans are equal and yet aggress against the basic needs of some humans whenever this serves our own nonbasic or luxury needs.[36] Consequently, if the equality of all living beings is to mean anything, it must be the case that the basic needs of nonhumans are protected against aggressive actions that only serve to meet the nonbasic needs of humans as is required by the Principle of Disproportionality.[37] Furthermore, substituting the Principle of Disproportionality here for Taylor's two principles enables us to successfully avoid the apparent inconsistency between Taylor's priority principles and his theory.[38]

Taylor has two other priority principles. They are:

> *A Principle of Distributive Justice*
> This principle requires that when the interests of the parties are all basic ones and there exists a natural source of good that can be used for the benefit of any of the parties, each party must be allotted an equal share.

> *A Principle of Restitutive Justice*
> This principle requires that whenever the principle of minimal wrong has been followed or the principle of distributive justice has been imperfectly followed, some form of reparation or compensation is called for if our actions are to be fully consistent with the attitude of respect for nature.

Unfortunately, by requiring equal shares, Taylor's Principle of Distributive Justice is far too demanding, even as a principle applying only to humans, let alone as a principle of interspecies ethics. When basic needs are at stake the Principles of Human Defense and Human Preservation impose more reasonable requirements. Accordingly, we should simply discard Taylor's Principle of Distributive Justice, and so avoid the charge of being too demanding.

In addition, given the changes in the other principles, biocentric pluralism requires a different principle of restitution. It is:

> *A Principle of Restitution*
> Appropriate reparation or compensation is required whenever the other principles have been violated.

Obviously, this principle, like Taylor's Principle of Restitutive Justice, is somewhat vague, but for people who are willing to abide by the other three priority principles, it should be possible to remedy that vagueness in practice.

At this point, it might be objected that my reformulation of Taylor's environmentalism has not taken sufficiently into account the conflict between holists and individualists. According to holists, the good of a species or the good of an ecosystem or the good of the whole biotic community can trump the good of individual living beings.[39] According to individualists, the good of each individual living thing must be respected.[40]

Now one might think that holists would require that we abandon my Principle of Human Preservation. Yet consider. Assuming that people's basic needs are at stake, how could it be morally objectionable for them to try to meet those needs, even if this were to harm nonhuman individuals, or species, or whole ecosystems, or even, to some degree, the whole biotic community?[41] Of course, we can *ask* people in such conflict cases not to meet their basic needs in order to prevent harm to nonhuman individuals or species, ecosystems or the whole biotic community. But if people's basic needs are at stake, we cannot reasonably demand that they make such a sacrifice. We could demand, of course, that people do all that they reasonably can to keep such conflicts from arising in the first place, for, just as in traditional ethics, many severe conflicts of interest can be avoided simply by doing what is morally required early on.[42] Nevertheless, when people's basic needs are at stake, the individualist perspective seems incontrovertible. We cannot reasonably require people to be saints.[43]

At the same time, when people's basic needs are not at stake, we would be justified in acting on holistic grounds to prevent serious harm to nonhuman individuals, or species, or ecosystems, or the whole biotic community. Obviously, it will be difficult to know when our interventions will have this effect, but when we can be reasonably sure that they will, such interventions (e.g., culling elk herds in wolf-free ranges or preserving the habitat of endangered species) would be morally permissible, and maybe even morally required.[44] This shows that it is possible to agree with individualists when the basic needs of human beings are at stake, and to agree with holists when they are not.

Yet this combination of individualism and holism appears to conflict with the equality of species by imposing greater sacrifices on the members of nonhuman species than it does on the members of the human species. Fortunately, appearances are deceiving here. Although the proposed resolution only justifies imposing holism when people's basic needs are not at stake, it does not justify imposing individualism at all.[45] Rather, it would simply permit individualism when people's basic needs *are* at stake. Of course, we could impose holism under all conditions. But given that this would, in effect, involve going to war against people who are simply striving to meet their own basic needs in the only way they can, as permitted by the Principle of Human Preservation, intervention in such cases would not be justified. It would involve taking away the means of survival from people, even when these means are not required for one's own survival.[46]

Nevertheless, this combination of individualism and holism may leave animal liberationists wondering about the further implications of this resolution for the treatment of animals. Obviously, a good deal of work has already been done on this topic. Initially, philosophers thought that humanism could be extended to include animal liberation and eventually environmental holism.[47] Then Baird Callicott argued that animal liberation and environmental holism were as opposed to each other as they were to humanism.[48] The resulting conflict Callicott called "a triangular affair." Agreeing with Callicott, Mark Sagoff contended that any attempt to link together animal liberation and environmental holism would lead to "a bad marriage and a quick divorce."[49] Yet more recently, such philosophers as Mary Ann Warren have tended to play down the opposition between animal liberation and environmental holism, and even Callicott now thinks he can bring the two back together again.[50] There are good reasons for thinking that such a reconciliation is possible.

Right off, it would be good for the whole environment if people generally, especially people in the first world, adopted a more vegetarian diet of the sort that animal liberationists are recommending. This is because a good portion of livestock production today consumes grains that could be more effectively used for direct human consumption. For example, 90 percent of the protein, 99 percent of the carbohydrate, and 100 percent of the fiber value of grain is wasted by cycling it through livestock, and currently 30 percent of worldwide production of grain and 70 percent of U.S. production is fed to livestock.[51] So by adopting a more vegetarian diet, people generally, especially people in the first world, could significantly reduce the amount of farmland that has to be kept in production to feed the human population. This, in turn, could have beneficial effects on the whole biotic community by eliminating the amount of soil erosion and environmental pollutants that result from raising livestock. For example, it has been estimated that 85 percent of U.S. topsoil lost from cropland, pasture, range land, and forest land is directly associated with raising livestock.[52] So, along with preventing animal suffering, there are these additional reasons to favor a more vegetarian diet.[53]

But even though a more vegetarian diet seems in order, it is not clear that we would be morally required to become complete vegetarians. Sagoff assumes that in a completely vegetarian human world people would continue to feed farm animals as before.[54] But it is not clear that we would have any obligation to do so. Moreover, in a completely vegetarian human world, unless production is increased considerably, we would probably need most of the grain we now feed livestock to meet the still unmet nutritional needs of people, particularly in developing countries. There simply would not be enough grain to go around. And there would also be the need to conserve cropland for future generations. So in a completely vegetarian human world, it seems likely that the population of farm animals would be decimated, relegating many of the farm animals that remain to zoos. On this account, it may be morally permissible for us to raise farm animals under healthy conditions, hence not in the numbers sustainable only with factory farms, but then kill them relatively painlessly and eat them, rather than that they not be maintained at all.[55] Presumably this would be the kind of arrangement that a human advocate for farm animals who was behind a veil of ignorance would choose for them, knowing that humans would be only under an obligation to maintain a few farm animals in zoos unless some mutually beneficial arrangement was established. So a completely vegetarian human world would not seem to be morally required.[56]

Nor, it seems, would it be in the interest of wild species who no longer have their natural predators not to be hunted by humans, or at least culled by expert shooters.[57] Of course, where possible, it may be preferable to reintroduce natural predators. But this may not always be possible because of the proximity of farm animals and human populations; in such cases, if action is not taken to control the populations of wild species, disaster could result for the species and their environments. For example, deer, rabbits, squirrels, quails, and ducks reproduce rapidly, and in the absence of predators can quickly exceed the carrying capacity of their environments. So it may be in the interest of certain wild species and their environments that humans intervene periodically to cull their populations to maintain a balance. Of course, there will be many natural environments where it is in the interest of the environment and the wild animals that inhabit it to be simply left alone. But here too animal liberation and environmental holism would not be in conflict. For these reasons, animal liberationists would have little reason to object to the proposed combination of individualism and holism within biocentric pluralism.

Of course, there are interpretations of animal liberation for which there is a conflict with environmental holism. In biocentric pluralism, the grounds for animal liberation is the absence of any non-question-begging argument for human superiority or domination, and this holds for plants, species, and ecosystems as well as for individual animals. But if one takes the grounds for animal liberation to be the similarity of animals to humans, as Regan and, to a lesser degree, Singer do, then the requirement to benefit individual animals can be quite strong, resulting in significant conflicts with environmental holism. In biocentric pluralism, our obligation to most nonhuman living beings, especially wild ones, unlike our obligation to fellow humans, is simply to leave them alone.

For the most part, we are required to do good to nonhuman living beings only when restitution is required. In addition, it will frequently be the case that any help we would give to some nonhuman living beings would be harmful to others, or to species or ecosystems and, for that reason, should not be done. By contrast, in Regan's view and, to a lesser degree, in Singer's, since species and ecosystems don't count morally, and since the obligation to do good or prevent harm to individual animals is quite strong, we can be frequently required to intervene, for example, between predator and prey, in ways that conflict with the requirements of environmental holism.[58] Thus, biocentric pluralism, unlike Regan's and Singer's views, succeeds in supporting animal liberation without conflicting with environmental holism.

It might still be objected that for all that has been said so far, my defense of biocentric pluralism still faces an unresolvable dilemma. The dilemma is this: Either biocentric pluralism holds to its claim that all species are equal or it gives up that claim. If it holds to the claim that all species are equal, it imposes an unreasonable sacrifice on humans. If it gives up that claim to avoid imposing an unreasonable sacrifice on humans, it is committed to an indefensible anthropocentricism. Either way, biocentric pluralism should be rejected. Actually, I think that it is possible to grasp both horns of this dilemma, but here I have only been concerned to grasp the first.[59]

My argument has been that to grasp the first horn of the dilemma, we need to understand the equality of species by analogy with the equality of humans. We need to see that just as we claim that humans are equal but then justifiably treat them differently, so too we can claim that all species are equal but justifiably treat them differently as well. In traditional ethics, various interpretations are given to human equality that allow for different treatment of humans. In ethical egoism, everyone is *equally at liberty* to pursue his or her own interests, but this allows us always to prefer ourselves to others, who are understood to be like opponents in a competitive game. In libertarianism, everyone has an *equal right* to liberty, but although this imposes some limits on the pursuit of self-interest, it is said to allow us to refrain from helping others in severe need. In welfare liberalism, everyone has an *equal right* to welfare and opportunity, but this need not commit us to providing everyone with exactly the same resources. In socialism, everyone has an *equal right* to self-development, and although this may commit us to providing everyone with the same resources, it still sanctions some degree of self-preference. So just as there are various ways to interpret human equality that still allow us to treat humans differently, there are various ways that we can interpret species equality that allow us to treat species differently.

Now those who would object to biocentric pluralism appear to be interpreting species equality in a very strong sense, analogous to the interpretation of equality found in socialism. But the kind of species equality that I have defended is more akin to the equality found in welfare liberalism or in libertarianism than it is to the equality found in socialism. In brief, this form of equality requires that we not aggress against the basic needs of the members of other species for the sake of the nonbasic needs of the members of our own species (the Principle of Disproportionality), but it permits us to aggress against the basic needs of the members of other species for the sake of the basic needs of the members of our own species (the Principle of Human Preservation); and it also permits us to defend the basic and even the nonbasic needs of the members of our own species against harmful aggression by members of other species (the Principle of Human Defense).

Furthermore, the claim of species equality, like the claim of human equality, is simply the claim that all species, like all human beings, are the same in one relevant respect—that they should count morally. It does not maintain that they are the same (equal) in other respects, or that they should be treated the same (equally) in all respects. In this way, biocentric pluralism allows us to accept the claim of species equality while avoiding imposing an unreasonable sacrifice on the members of our own species, and thereby grasp the first horn of the dilemma raised against biocentric pluralism as a morally defensible form of environmentalism.[60]

The Response of Traditional Ethics

How should traditional ethics respond to this challenge of environmentalism, particularly in the form of biocentric pluralism? There are at least four responses, each of which, if valid, would suffice to answer this challenge. The first response is that environmentalism is too demanding to be morally required. The second response is that environmentalism is based on an unjustifiable leap from facts to values or from "is" to "ought." The third is that the domination of nonhuman nature can be shown to be morally justified on religious grounds. The fourth is that environmentalism is unnecessary because the same or similar requirements can be derived from a completely human-centered environmental ethics. Let us take up each of these responses in turn.

Actually, the first response that environmentalism, particularly in the form of biocentric pluralism, is too demanding has already been dealt with. Thus, in setting out the view, I argued that "we cannot reasonably require people to be saints," that we need to avoid "imposing a unreasonable sacrifice on the members of our own species" and I even rejected one of Taylor's priority principles because I claimed it was "too demanding." Moreover, the main rationale for modifying Taylor's view was to come up with a consistent set of priority principles that were demanding but not *too demanding*. Moreover, as we have seen, just as traditional ethics permits a certain degree of preference for ourselves and those we care about while maintaining the equality of humans, or that humans count morally, biocentric pluralism permits a certain degree of preference for humans over nonhuman nature while maintaining the equality of species, or that other species count morally. All that biocentric pluralism prohibits is aggressing against the basic needs of nonhuman nature merely to satisfy the nonbasic or luxury needs of ourselves or other humans beings.

The second response to the challenge of environmentalism is that it involves an unjustifiable leap from facts to values or from "is" to "ought." Given that biocentric pluralism claims that all living beings should count morally because they have a good of their own, this would seem to involve a derivation of "values" from "facts" in such a way that we can always ask why these "facts" and not others are the grounds for the derivation.[61] Of course, animal liberationists, who hold that only sentient beings or experiencing subjects of life count morally, and most people, who appear to be anthropocentrists and hold that only humans or, more generally, rational beings count morally, face the same problem. But is there any way out of this problem?

Clearly, our basic ethical concern is to determine the prerogatives of and constraints on us in our relationship with other living beings. The prerogatives specify the ways that we can justifiably harm nonhuman living beings (the Principles of Human Defense and Human Preservation) while the constraints specify the ways that we cannot justifiably harm them (the Principle of Disproportionality). Now it is important to notice that the constraints specifying ways that we should not harm other living beings are simply requirements that, under certain conditions, we should leave other living beings alone, that is, not interfere with them. They are not requirements that we do anything for them. To generally require that we do something beneficial for nonhuman living beings (except when restitution is required) would be to require much more of us. It would entail positive obligations to benefit nonhuman living beings, not just negative obligations not to harm them by interfering with them. In general, this would be to demand too much from us, in effect, requiring us to be saints, and, as we have noted before, morality is not in the business of requiring us to be saints. Accordingly, the general obligation of noninterference that we have with respect to nonhuman living beings is fixed not so much by the nature of those other living beings as by what constraints or requirements can be reasonably imposed on ourselves.[62] Thus, we can see that those who benefit from the obligations that can be reasonably imposed on ourselves must have a certain independence to their lives; they must be able to get along on their own, without the help of others. In other words, they must have a good of their own.[63]

Accordingly, I have specified the class of those nonhumans to which we can have moral obligations not primarily in terms of the factual characteristics of those to whom we have those obligations, but rather in terms of what constraints or requirements can reasonably be imposed on us in this regard.[64] This is not a derivation of values from facts or of "ought" from "is" where we can always ask why these facts and not some others support the derivation. Rather, it is a derivation of values from values or of "ought" from "ought" where the necessity of the derivation can be displayed.

We can more clearly display this derivation by the following argument:

(1) The requirements of morality are reasonable to impose on human beings.
(2) The Principles of Human Defense, Human Preservation, Disproportionality, and Restitution, in contrast with the alternatives, are reasonable to impose on human beings.
(3) The Principles of Human Defense, Human Preservation, Disproportionality, and Restitution are requirements of morality.

Since the basic premise of this argument (1) is widely accepted as a fundamental characterization of morality, I think that the conclusion (3) can clearly be seen to follow.[65] Of course, a fuller statement of this argument would require an elaboration of the considerations that I have advanced in this chapter.[66] Nevertheless, I think that I have said enough to indicate how biocentric pluralism avoids an unjustifiable leap from facts to values.

Turning to the third response to the challenge of environmentalism, many people have appealed to the creation story in Genesis to show that domination of nonhuman nature is morally justified on religious grounds. In one version of this story, God tells humans to

> be fruitful and multiply, and fill the earth and subdue it. Have dominion over the fish of the sea, the birds of the air, cattle, and all the animals that crawl on the earth. (Genesis 1:28)

One interpretation of this directive is that humans are required or permitted to dominate nonhuman nature, that is, to use animals and plants for whatever purposes we happen to have, giving no independent weight at all to the interests of animals and plants. They are simply means to our ends.[67] Another interpretation, however, understands dominion not as domination but as a caring stewardship toward nonhuman nature, which imposes limits on the ways that we can use animals and plants in pursuit of our own purposes, thereby making it possible for other living things to flourish.[68]

Obviously, this second interpretation accords better with the perspective of biocentric pluralism. However, it is the first interpretation that is most widely accepted throughout Western culture. Yet given these conflicting interpretations of the Genesis story, it is clear that an appeal to the Bible is not going to be decisive in determining how anyone should treat nonhuman nature. What should be decisive in this context, however, is an argument based on reason alone for favoring biocentric pluralism over the domination of nonhuman nature. Fortunately, we have such an argument. As we have seen, biocentric pluralism is rationally preferable to the domination of nonhuman nature when judged from a non-question-begging standpoint just as in traditional ethics morality is rationally preferable to ethical egoism when judged from a non-question-begging standpoint (see chapter 1). In both cases, reason alone favors a non-question-begging resolution.

The fourth response to the challenge of environmentalism is that there is no need to endorse the view, because the same or similar requirements can be derived from a completely human-centered environmental ethics. According to this response, there is a happy coincidence between what is for the overall good of present generations of humans and what is for the overall good of all other living beings, or at least a happy coincidence between what is for the overall good of present and *future* generations of humans and what is for the overall good of all other present and future living beings.

But is this the case? No doubt, with respect to some environmental problems, like global warming and ozone depletion, a significant coincidence of interest exists,[69] but with respect to other environmental problems, such as endangered species, it would be surprising if a coincidence of interest between humans and nonhumans always obtained, even when the good of future generations

of human beings is taken into account. We surely recognize conflicts of interests between humans. Yet the possibility of conflict
is even greater between different species and the members of different species. So to hypothesize a coincidence of interest in all such
cases in order to be able to deny the need for priority principles is
simply to fly in the face of reality. Accordingly, morally defensible priority or conflict-resolution principles, like those of biocentric pluralism, are definitely needed to reasonably resolve conflicts
of interest between human and nonhuman nature. Moreover, even
when there is no conflict between what is for the good of humans
and what is for the overall good of nonhuman nature, it will sometimes be necessary to appeal to bio-centered justifications if we are
to overcome human selfishness and secure the right kind of behavior, just as in society it is still sometimes necessary to appeal
to both the law and morality to overcome human selfishness and
secure the right kind of behavior.[70] Hence, the need for environmentalism, particularly in the form of biocentric pluralism, is about
as great as it gets if we hope to put morality into practice.

So it turns out that none of the four responses to the challenge
of environmentalism in the form of biocentric pluralism is successful. In the absence of a cogent response, therefore, we have no
reasonable alternative open to us but to accept the challenge of environmentalism and modify traditional ethics to accord with its
demands. This requires accepting the Principles of Human Defense, Human Preservation, Disproportionality, and Restitution as
the appropriate priority or conflict-resolution principles to resolve
conflicts between humans and nonhuman nature. Only by thus incorporating these principles into traditional ethics will we be giving the challenge of environmentalism its due.

3

FEMINISM

The Masculine Bias in Traditional Ethics and How to Correct It

The failure of traditional ethics to sufficiently take into account the interests of women is what gives rise to the feminist challenge that traditional ethics is biased in favor of men. Recent interest in this challenge dates from the publication of Carol Gilligan's *In a Different Voice* in 1982.[1] In this chapter, I will argue that this bias of traditional ethics is manifested by the practical inadequacy of (1) its theories of justice, (2) its public/private distinction, and (3) its ideals of a morally good person. I will also suggest in each case how this bias can be corrected.[2]

The Practical Inadequacy of Traditional Theories of Justice

In her influential work *In a Different Voice,* Gilligan argues against the then prevailing view that women's moral development tends to lag behind that of men. According to Gilligan, men and women do tend to make different moral judgments, but there is no basis for claiming that the moral judgments of men are better than the moral judgments of women. All we can justifiably say is that they are different.

Gilligan goes on to contrast a care perspective favored by women with a justice perspective favored by men. According to Gilligan, these two perspectives are analogous to the alternative ways we tend to organize ambiguous perceptual patterns, for example, seeing a figure first as a square, then as a diamond depending upon its relationship to the surrounding frame. More specifically, Gilligan claims:

> From a justice perspective, the self as moral agent stands as the figure against a ground of social relationships, judging the conflicting claims of self and others against a standard of equality or equal respect (the Categorical Imperative, the Golden Rule). From a care perspective, the relationship becomes the figure, defining self and others. Within the context of relationship, the self as a moral agent perceives and responds to the perception of need. The shift in moral perspective is manifest by a change in the moral question from "What is just?" to "How to respond?"[3]

Using these perspectives as classificatory tools, Gilligan reports that 69 percent of her sample raised considerations of both justice and care while 67 percent focused their attention on one set of concerns (with focus defined as 75 percent or more of the considerations raised pertaining either to justice or to care). Significantly, with one exception, all of the men in the latter group focused on justice. The women were divided, with roughly one-third focusing on care and one-third on justice.[4] The conclusion that Gilligan draws from this research is that the care perspective is an equally valid moral perspective that has tended to be disregarded in moral theory and psychological research alike because of male bias.

Critics, however, have questioned to what degree Gilligan has succeeded in specifying two contrasting perspectives.[5] At one point, Gilligan characterizes the justice perspective by the injunction "do not act unfairly toward others" and the care perspective by the injunction "Do not turn away from someone in need."[6] But these two injunctions are inextricably linked in some conceptions of justice. For example, in a welfare-liberal conception of justice with its ideal of fairness, to treat people fairly is to respond to their needs.

Sometimes Gilligan defends her distinction between a justice perspective and a care perspective by characterizing a justice perspective in an even more restrictive way as simply requiring a right of noninterference and a corresponding duty of others not to interfere.[7] Similarly, the editors of a collection of essays inspired by Gilligan's work contend that in a justice perspective, "People are surely entitled to noninterference; they may not be entitled to aid."[8] But this is to identify a justice perspective with a libertarian view that purports to reject rights to welfare and equal opportunity. Thus, this characterization of a justice perspective again fails to countenance other conceptions of justice, such as a welfare-liberal conception of justice or a socialist conception of justice, whose requirements clearly go beyond a right to noninterference.

Now it may be objected that while some justice perspectives might be shown to accord with the requirements of a care perspective, they cannot always do so, and, in at least some cases, where the two perspectives are in conflict, the care perspective can be seen to have priority over the justice perspective.

Virginia Held offers us an example of what she takes to be just such a case in which care has priority over justice.[9] A father of a young child is also a teacher with a special skill in helping troubled young children succeed academically. If this father devotes most of his time to helping troubled young children and lets his wife and others care for his own child, he will accomplish a lot of good. Even if the father takes into account the amount of good he can accomplish by spending more time with his own child, the good he will accomplish by devoting more time to helping troubled young children succeed academically is far greater. Nevertheless, Held thinks that this is a case where the care perspective, which requires that the father spend more time with his child, has priority over the justice perspective, which requires that he spend more time helping troubled young children succeed academically.

Yet even supposing Held was right about the particular moral requirements in this case, it is not clear that this is a case where care has priority over justice. As Claudia Card has pointed out, it is possible to view the father's requirement to spend more time with his child as a requirement of (particular) justice.[10] Imagine that the child deserves more attention from his father, and that (particular) justice requires the father to give the child what he or she deserves. So construed, this would be a case where a requirement of (particular) justice has priority over the requirement of (universal) justice to help others in need.[11] Again, what this example illustrates is how difficult it is to distinguish between a justice perspective and a care perspective.

We can, of course, distinguish between a universalist perspective, which grounds our obligations to others in their having the same moral status as ourselves, and a particularist perspective, which grounds our obligations to others in the particular relationships and commitments we have to those others. A universalist perspective gives us, among other things, an obligation to respect the basic rights of other persons, while the particularist perspective gives us, among other things, an obligation to honor our parents. Yet within both of these perspectives, considerations of justice and care can be found. The requirements of justice that derive from a universalist perspective require us to *care* for others, at least to the degree necessary to carry out those requirements. For example, from a universalist welfare-liberal perspective, we are required to secure a basic minimum for the poor. And the same holds true with respect to the requirements of justice that derive from a particularist perspective. They too require us to *care* for others, at least to the degree necessary to carry out those requirements. For example, from a particularist perspective, we are required to be of special assistance to our friends when they are in need.

Moreover, within both perspectives, justice can restrict care as well as demand it. People can care too much in ways that are harmful to themselves or others, as when parents spoil their children. Further, care that is neither restricted nor demanded by justice is permitted to go beyond it in many ways, as we expect to happen in loving relationships.

Now when conflicts arise between the requirements of a universalist and a particularist perspective, they can be viewed as conflicts between justice and (morally appropriate) care, but they can also be viewed as conflicts between (particular) justice and (universal) justice, as Card argued was true of Held's example.[12] So distinguishing between a universalist and a particularist perspective will not help us to distinguish between justice and care because considerations of justice and care are found within both perspectives.[13]

But if we can't distinguish in theory between a justice perspective and a care perspective, it is going to be impossible for researchers to use this distinction in practice to characterize people as focusing on one or the other perspective. Of course, people will tend to use the language of justice and rights with the frequencies Gilligan observes, but we will have to look behind this usage to see what people are claiming when they use or don't use this language. If there is no viable theoretical distinction between a justice perspective and a care perspective, people frequently will be found to express care and concern for the needs of others by using the language of justice and rights as well as by using the language of care.

Nevertheless, even if we cannot draw a viable theoretical distinction between a justice perspective and a care perspective, because at least some conceptions of justice are quite capable of expressing care and concern for the needs of others, it is still possible to raise a feminist challenge to traditional ethics in this regard at the practical level. This is because even theoretically adequate conceptions of justice tend to be applied in practice in ways that do not properly take into account the interests of women.

Take, for example, John Rawls's theory of justice. Working within the Kantian tradition, Rawls maintains, as we noted before, that principles of justice are those principles that persons behind an imaginary veil of ignorance would unanimously agree should be followed. This imaginary veil extends to most of the particular facts about oneself—anything that would bias one's choice or stand in the way of a unanimous agreement. It masks one's knowledge of one's social position, talents, sex, race, and religion, but not one's knowledge of such general information as would be contained in political, social, economic, and psychological theories. Persons in this original position, Rawls claims, would choose certain principles of justice because they assume, among other things, that they have the capacity for what Rawls calls "a sense of justice," that is, the capacity to abide by the principles of justice they have chosen.[14] In Rawls's theory, this assumption of a capacity for "a sense of justice" is further grounded in the assumption that persons in his original position have been raised in just families.[15] But while Rawls thus grounds his principles of justice in the possibility of just families, Rawls himself, until very recently (1997)—more than twenty-five years after he published his monumental *A Theory of Justice*—had published nothing about the nature of just families. Since Rawls has clarified and developed his theory of justice in many ways since the publication of *A Theory of Justice,* culminating in the publication of his second book, *Political Liberalism,* in 1993, one can only conclude that Rawls did not think that it was very important to the defense of his theory to specify the nature of just families.[16]

From a feminist standpoint, however, the absence of any account of the nature of just families is a significant failing for a theory of justice.[17] When you consider that in the United States almost 20 percent of children live in poverty, that we share with Italy the highest infant mortality rate in the industrialized world, and, except for Bolivia and Haiti, have the lowest vaccination rate for children under the age of two in the Western Hemisphere, that each day 135,000 children take a gun to school, that one in seven claim to have been sexually abused as a child, that the home is actually a more dangerous place for women than the city streets, that typically more women are abused by their husbands than get married in a given year, that one-third of all women who require emergency hospital treatment are there as a result of domestic violence, that 50 percent of first marriages and 60 percent of second marriages are likely to end in divorce, that 42 percent of children whose father had left the marriage had not seen him in the past year, it should be apparent that we need an account of the nature of just families.[18] Even if a particular theory of justice has the resources to develop an adequate account of the nature and structure of just families, the failure of its defenders to actually do so creates the presumption that existing family structures are morally acceptable when, as many feminists have argued, they are, in fact, biased in favor of men.[19]

Belatedly, in a recent article, devoted largely to another topic, Rawls does include a section entitled "On the Family as Part of the Basic Structure," where he takes up the question of what implications his conception of justice has for family life.[20] Here Rawls argues that "since wives have all the same basic rights, liberties and opportunities as their husbands, this should secure their equality and independence."[21] Nevertheless, he also argues that his conception of justice

> may have to allow for some traditional gendered division of labor within families . . . provided it is fully voluntary and does not result from or lead to . . . other forms of discrimination elsewhere in the social system [which make] it rational and less costly for husband and wife to follow a gendered division of labor in the family.[22]

Now the division of labor within families is gendered, and, in general, families themselves are gendered when the assignment of roles is made on the basis of sex or sex socialization.[23] In gendered families, one has the roles one has because of one's sex or because one has been socialized in a certain way because of one's sex. Thus, the fact that Rawls believes that gendered families can be compatible with his conception of justice may help explain why he did not address the question of the nature of just families earlier. If gendered families can be just, there is no urgency to providing an account of just families as long as many of the gendered families that presently exist turn out to be just.

Yet, at least in the United States, to guarantee equal opportunity for women and men would require that we continue to radically modify traditional family structures. Given that a significant proportion of the available jobs are at least nine-to-five, families with preschool children require day care facilities if their adult members are to pursue their careers. Unfortunately, for many families such facilities are simply unavailable. In New York City, for example, day care providers have waiting lists totaling between 35,000 and 40,000 children, and it is projected that an additional 109,000 children will need day care by 2001. In Seattle, there is licensed day care space for only 8,800 of the 23,000 children who need it. In Los Angeles, there is no licensed child care available for

135,000 children who need such programs. In Woodbridge, New Jersey, a single, twenty-four year-old mother was arrested for leaving her five-year-old daughter unattended in a parked car while she worked the night shift at a local mall. But when it was discovered that she was unable to find any child care and was working hard to support herself and her daughter without any assistance from her former husband, all serious charges against her were dismissed.[24]

Moreover, even the available day care facilities in the United States are frequently inadequate, either because their staffs are poorly trained or because the child/adult ratio in such facilities is too high. Child-care workers are in the lowest tenth of all wage earners, well below janitors. They frequently get no health insurance or other benefits, which makes child care an even less attractive job. At the average day care center, the personnel turnover rate is 41 percent a year.[25] Even though poor families spend an estimated 25 percent of their income on day care, many such facilities provide little more than custodial care at best; at worst, they actually retard the development of the children in their care.[26] What this suggests is that at least in the absence of adequate day care facilities, if preschool children are to be appropriately cared for, frequently one of the adult members of the family has to remain at home to provide that care. But because most jobs are at least 9 to 5, this requires that the adult members who stay at home temporarily give up pursuing a career. However, such sacrifice conflicts with the equal opportunity requirement of Rawls's conception of justice.

Families might try to meet this equal opportunity requirement by having one parent relinquish a career for a certain period of time and the other give up pursuing a career for a subsequent (equal) period of time. But there are problems here too. Some careers are difficult to interrupt for any significant period of time, while others never adequately reward latecomers. In addition, given the high rate of divorce and the inadequacies of most legally mandated child support, those who first sacrifice their careers may find themselves later faced with the impossible task of trying to begin or revive them while continuing to be the primary caretakers of their children.[27] Furthermore, there is considerable evidence that children benefit more from equal rearing from both parents.[28] So the option of having just one parent doing the child rearing for any length of time is, other things being equal, not optimal.

It would seem, therefore, that to truly share child rearing within the family what is needed are flexible (typically part-time) work schedules that allow both parents to be together with their children for a significant period every day. Some flexible work schedules have already been tried by various corporations in the United States. For example, Du Pont has 2,000 employees working part time and between 10,000 and 15,000 working flextime, and IBM has a "flexible work leave of absence" plan that allows employees to work up to three years part time and still collect full-time employment benefits.[29] Unfortunately, the U.S. Family Leave Act of 1993 mandates only twelve weeks of unpaid leave and that only for companies with more than fifty employees. In addition, the Act covers only 5 percent of all firms and only 60 percent of all workers, and according to one study, only 40 percent of working women can take advantage of the full unpaid leave without severe financial hardship.[30] By contrast, in Canada employees receive fifteen weeks at 60 percent pay, and in Sweden employees receive thirty-six weeks at 90 percent pay and prorated paid leave for the next eighteen months.[31] In fact, the United States is only one of six of 152 nations surveyed by the UN that does not require paid maternity leave.[32] But if equal opportunity is to be a reality, the option of paid family leave and flexible work schedules must be guaranteed to all those with preschool children. A recent estimate also shows that married full-time career women still do almost as much of the housework—70 percent—as the average full-time housewife, who does 83 percent.[33] Obviously this too would have to change if we are to achieve the ideal of equal opportunity for men and women.

But what about Rawls's claim that it is possible for there to be gendered families that are consistent with the ideal of equal opportunity for men and women, and, hence, just? In an attempt to support Rawls's claim that gendered families can still be just, Sharon Lloyd has offered two cases.[34] In the first, a couple dream of amassing sufficient savings to be able to retire early and sail around the world for the rest of their days. To achieve this goal, the husband devotes himself exclusively to developing and utilizing a rare talent in a job more lucrative than any other that either he or his wife could obtain, and she single-handedly cares for the family and raises the children during their formative years. In the other case, a wife wants to live in a grand house and enjoy an expensive lifestyle while her husband prefers modest lodgings and a less costly lifestyle. As a compromise, the couple decide to buy the grand house with the understanding that the wife will work harder and longer than her husband to pay for the more expensive lifestyle she wanted.

So has Lloyd provided us with cases of gendered families that are just? Actually, the cases are not fully specified enough to make a determination. Whether families are gendered or not depends on the opportunities that are available to women and men in the societies in which they live. If equal opportunities are truly available to women and men both inside and outside family structures, then families in that society are not gendered, because the assignment of roles in that society is not made on the basis of sex or sex socialization. Accordingly, if women and men have equal opportunities in the families that Lloyd describes, those families would not be gendered. It is impossible for there to be gendered families in a society where there are equal opportunities for women and men, because the assignment of roles in that society would be on the basis of those opportunities, people's natural abilities, and their free choices. In a nongendered society, women and men would have equal opportunity to develop whatever natural abilities they have to fulfill the roles within that society in accord with their free choices. Notice too that children raised in such a society in families of the sort that Lloyd describes would not view their parents' distinctive roles as gender roles but rather as roles they freely chose within the context of equal opportunity for women and men.

Of course, given that one's sex does determine at least some of one's natural abilities (for example, whether one may be able to bear a child), it does in this way figure into the assignment of roles even in a nongendered society. Nevertheless, an assignment of roles on the basis of equal opportunity, natural abilities, and free choice is still fundamentally different from an assignment on the basis of sex or sex socialization because in the latter assignment important non-sex-based natural abilities are ignored or slighted (for example, nurturance in the case of men and independence in the case of women), equal opportunity is not secured, and free choice is undermined. That is why an assignment of roles on the basis of sex or sex socialization is morally objectionable.

Richard Arneson, however, has questioned whether a society without gender roles can be characterized by a statistical equality between men and women such that in half the (heterosexual) marriages, men are the primary caretakers of children, and in the other half, women are the primary caretakers.[35] Actually, this would be very unlikely to obtain in a society where women and men have equal opportunities. Under such conditions, the expected norm for most families would be an equal sharing of roles both inside and outside of family structures, because that would be the normal way that women and men would develop themselves when the assignment of roles in a society is on the basis of equal opportunity, natural abilities, and free choice.[36] This means that cases of the sort Lloyd describes would turn out to be exceptions to this norm.

Even so, under a system of equal opportunity for women and men, could we not refer to roles that were still correlated with sex-based natural abilities as gender roles? For example, if it turns out that under a system of equal opportunity for women and men, women turn out to be most of the fighter pilots, now a premier role in the military, because of the shorter distance, on average, between head and heart, making them more capable of withstanding G-forces, and men turn out to be more of the grunt soldiers needed primarily for hand-to-hand combat, because of their average larger body size, could we not refer to such roles as gender roles?[37] We could, of course, do so, but it is not clear what would be the point of such a use of the term "gender roles," and certainly this usage would conflict with the normal understanding of gender roles as roles that are assigned on the basis of sex and sex socialization rather than on the basis of equal opportunity, natural abilities, and free choice.[38]

Hence, we are led to the conclusion that when Rawls's conception of justice is correctly applied to family structures, it rules out gendered families, as normally understood, as incompatible with equal opportunity for women and men. Unfortunately, the failure of Rawls, and most of the defenders of his view, to draw this conclusion shows how the practical application of his theory has, in fact, been biased in favor of men.

In this respect, however, contemporary defenders of utilitarian- or Aristotelian-based theories of justice have fared no better. In applying their theories, barring rare exceptions, they too have failed to recognize that their theories require gender-free societies in order to secure equal opportunity for both men and women.[39] So while their theories of justice are also theoretically adequate to take women's interests into account, utilitarians and Aristotelians have standardly applied their theories in ways that are, in fact, biased in favor of men. While the failure has been at the practical, not the theoretical, level, this failure at the practical level has unfortunately been widespread.

The problem is particularly severe because there is still so much inequality between men and women in society, and because most major figures in the history of ethics, such as Aristotle and Kant, have defended inequality of this sort as natural and right.[40] Consequently, the failure of contemporary moral philosophers to address and condemn this inequality between men and women when setting out their theories of justice shows a failure to take women's interests sufficiently into account and thus a bias against them.

The Practical Inadequacy of the Traditional Public/Private Distinction

The practical failure of traditional theories of justice to adequately take women's interests into account is related to the way the public/private distinction has been applied in traditional ethics.[41] The idea behind the public/private distinction is that there should be an area of life (a private domain) where people are free to make their own decisions and the force of the law would not be felt. This contrasts with an area of life (a public domain) where it is perfectly appropriate for the law to intervene and regulate and direct our lives. In theory, this distinction is a great idea. Surely there should be an area of our lives that is exempt from the force of the law, an area where we are free to do what we want without suffering legal penalties or liabilities. And, just as surely, there should be an area of our lives where we are justifiably subject to the law's jurisdiction. In practice, however, like theories of justice, this public/private distinction has been applied in ways that are biased in favor of men.

As the distinction is currently applied, at least in the United States, family life including the rearing of children is supposed to fall into the private area, the area exempt from the force of the law. But in practice, family life, including the rearing of children, has always been controlled by the law almost as much as the economy has been controlled by the law. For example, in 1745 the Massachusetts Assembly ordered that any child older than six who did not know the alphabet was to be removed to another family.[42] In the 1880s, the Illinois Supreme Court held that it was legal to indefinitely institutionalize any girl who begged or received alms while selling goods, regardless of her parents' wishes.[43] According to the U.S. Social Security Act of 1935 (revised in 1939), most women received benefits only through their husbands—and many discovered later that if the relationship lasted less than twenty years, they ended up with no benefits at all.[44] And as late as the 1970s, food stamps in the United States were denied to any poor family that shared cooking facilities with others.[45] So historically, at least in the United States, there has been the legal control of family life, which has been accompanied more recently by the denial that there is such control and by the denial of any need to publicly evaluate the nature of family life to determine how it should be controlled and regulated.

Nevertheless, once it is recognized that family life has, to a considerable degree, been controlled by the law, and thus, as such, has been in the public domain, the question arises whether legal control should continue, and, if so, how it should be exercised. Certainly, given the importance of the family to society, the legal control of family life does make sense. But if women's interests are to be adequately taken into account, a number of changes in the way that the law controls and regulates family life within the public domain are clearly required. I have already mentioned the need for adequate day care. In most Western European countries, day care is provided by law to all who request it.[46] The law should also be used to guarantee the provision of flextime to parents with preschool children and to mandate an effective mix of both paid and unpaid parental leave.

Furthermore, if family structures are to be just, there is a need to ensure that women's opportunities to work outside of the home are just as good as men's. To achieve this, the law needs to guarantee women and men equal access to equally good education and equally good jobs. In addition, the law should protect employees, primarily women, from various forms of sexual discrimination, particularly sexual harassment, so that women are employed under the same terms and conditions that men would be employed.[47] In the case of divorce, the law should also provide for an equitable division of marital assets and equitable support for children. This has been a serious problem, particularly in the United States.[48] Following divorce, women and children have usually experienced a significant drop in their standard of living while the standard of living of divorced men has improved.

It might be objected, however, that although the law should be used to regulate and control family life, using the law to help ensure equal opportunity between women and men is, in fact, destructive of traditional family life. But what are we to mean by a "traditional family" here? If we mean a family based on male breadwinning and female childrearing, then surely that sort of family is fast disappearing from Western societies. In the United States, for example, only 7 percent of families in 1986 were traditional families in that sense.[49] Moreover, the factor that has probably contributed most to the disappearance of the traditional family in the United States is not the opening up of greater opportunities to women but the declining income of single-income families. Consider that half the new jobs created in the United States in the 1980s paid a wage lower than the poverty figure for a family of four, that 40 percent of working wives are married to men earning less than $20,000 a year, and that more than one-third of all two-parent families would be poor if both parents did not work.[50] In any case, the current reality in the United States is that women are almost 50 percent of the paid labor force, and the question at issue is whether in this context we should be pursuing the goal of equal opportunity or fairness both inside and outside of family structures.[51]

Outside family structures, women and men working in the same job category sometimes have different incomes. For example, while female clerical workers in the United States earned a median wage of $384 per week in 1995, the median wage for male clerical workers was $489.[52] More frequently, however, women and men tend to be employed in different job categories that are paid differently. According to one study done in Denver, women employed as nurses earned less than men employed as tree cutters. According to another U.S. study, men employed as stockroom attendants earned more than women employed as dental hygienists. While in each of these cases, the women earned about 20 percent less than the men, the women's jobs, when evaluated in terms of skill, responsibility, effort, and working conditions, were given equal or higher scores than the men's jobs with which they were compared. But surely none of these ways of denying women the opportunity to earn the same as men do for equal or comparable work can be morally justified, and we need to design legal remedies for dealing with them, as has been done in some cases.[53]

But is there a similar justification for requiring equal opportunity or fairness inside family structures? Clearly, equal opportunity or fairness within the family would require that when both spouses are working full time in the paid labor force, then they both should equally share housekeeping and childrearing tasks, other things being equal. Otherwise, as so often happens, one spouse, almost always the wife, will end up with a second shift at home, which usually has detrimental effects on that spouse's work and well-being both inside and outside the family. Of course, when only one spouse is employed in the paid labor force, or only one spouse is working full time, then it is reasonable to expect that the other spouse will assume more of the housekeeping and childrearing responsibilities. However, in such cases, equal opportunity and fairness demand that in heterosexual families it should be no more reasonable to expect that it will be the woman who is assuming more of the housekeeping-childrearing responsibilities than it is to assume that it will be the man who is doing so.

So why not incorporate these requirements of equal opportunity and fairness within family structures? Sometimes it is argued that men lack the necessary housekeeping or childrearing skills owing to a deficient upbringing in which they were taught that housekeeping and childrearing are not appropriate activities for men to undertake.[54] But surely what this calls for is not the rejection of the standard of equal opportunity but rather the introduction of certain remedial programs to increase men's skills in this regard, in other words, affirmative action for men. This also points to the need to ensure that the early education of girls and boys within the family conforms to the standard of equal opportunity or fairness. If within families, girls are denied equal opportunities for development, if both girls and boys are taught that, irrespective of their natural abilities, certain roles and jobs should not be open to them because of their sex, this will surely make it more difficult to create and maintain equal opportunity or fairness between women and men later in life. Within families, then, other things being equal, girls and boys must also be given the same type of upbringing consistent with their native capabilities.

Now adequate day care, paid and unpaid parental leave, and flextime employment can all help to effect greater equal opportunity or fairness within the family, even in the face of male resistance, but still more needs to be done. We noted earlier that married full-time career women do almost as much of the housework as the average full-time housewife. Other studies in the United States show that men perceive doing an almost equal amount of housework—48 percent—*unfair* to themselves. According to these studies, men see the division as *fair* to both parties when they are doing 36 percent of the housework, and they only see the inequality as *unfair* when their wives are doing over 70 percent of the work.[55] We need, therefore, to try to correct these unfortunate misperceptions through such measures as required educational programs in our schools, including colleges and universities, publicly funded advertising analogous to the advertising directed against smoking, prohibiting gender-based advertising directed at children, and making the granting of marriage licenses conditional upon the completion of a special educational program that addresses the issue of equal opportunity and fairness in family life. In addition, public support, including tax-exempt status, should be denied to institutions and organizations such as private schools and churches that are not premised on equal opportunity for women and men. Obviously, implementing such measures will require that we relocate the public/private distinction in our lives, but if women are to have the same opportunities as men, there is no other practical alternative.

It might be objected, however, that at least within family structures, we should not use a standard of equal opportunity or fairness but rather one of love and affection. But a standard of love and affection that requires unfairness and imposes unequal burdens simply because of one's sex or sex socialization is *not* an adequate standard of love and affection. Love and affection within families can and should go beyond fairness or equal opportunity, but they should not go against them. Where there is proper love and affection, one doesn't need to demand fairness and equal opportunity. Rather these values are embraced as part of the way we have of showing proper love and affection for others. Thus, proper love and affection within the family would refuse to deny women equal opportunity on the basis of their sex or sex socialization.

In addition, if men and women are to have equal opportunity, we need to reduce the high incidence of violence perpetrated against women, in the forms of rape, assault, and sexual abuse. To do that, we will need to further relocate the public/private distinction in our lives. Thus, in addition to the usual ways that the law should be strengthened to make it easier to prosecute and convict offenders, it would also help to ban hard-core pornography that celebrates and legitimizes rape, battery, and the sexual abuse of children. Catharine MacKinnon has argued that pornography of this sort goes beyond mere speech in constituting a practice of sex discrimination that is a violation of women's civil rights.[56] While the consumption of pornography has been thought to belong to the private domain, MacKinnon has argued that pornography has public effects on the lives of women that require a coercive corrective. According to MacKinnon, men who consume pornography learn through the pleasures of masturbation to enjoy the forceful subordination of women, and they seek to find ways to impose that same subordination on the women who come into their lives. Because of the severity of these impositions, MacKinnon and other antipornography feminists claim that hard-core pornography violates women's civil rights by denying their equal status as citizens.[57] Of course, it can be questioned whether the impositions that are inflicted on women by hard-core pornography are actually severe enough to justify its prohibition. Here MacKinnon and other antipornography feminists cite studies showing that exposure to hard-core pornography increases discriminatory attitudes and behavior in men toward women that take both violent and nonviolent forms.[58] Other studies reveal that in 68 percent of 2,380 cases, the abuser beat or sexually abused the victim or someone else after looking at pornographic material, and that 58 percent of abusers point out pornographic pictures or articles to their victims.[59]

Moreover, given that the enjoyment of hard-core pornography comes from vicariously experiencing and identifying with the activity of forcefully subordinating women, it is difficult to see how men can experience such enjoyment, culminating in orgasm, without desiring to actually forcefully subordinate women in real life.

To see how difficult it would be for men not to be moved to desire in such contexts, suppose we inhabited a world in which in all the fiction we encounter, the morally bad characters, who always look attractive, triumph over the morally good characters, who always look unattractive. Imagine that in this fiction, glorified Hitlers and Stalins always triumph over disparaged Gandhis and Jesuses. In such a world, how could we think that the fiction to which people were exposed would not move them to desire to act like the morally bad characters? Moreover, can you imagine what strong corrective measures many people would want to take if the poetic justice of fiction began to be reversed in this fashion?

And would not the reason those people would give for taking such strong corrective measures be that this reversal of poetic justice would lead people to behave similarly in real life?

Why then would not a similar justification be given for banning hard-core pornography, since it involves a similar reversal of poetic justice with the morally bad characters (in this case, men generally), who appear strong and dominant, triumphing over the morally good characters (in this case, women generally) who appear weak and submissive? It might be argued that the difference between the imaginary world, where there is a recognized need for some corrective action to restore poetic justice, and our own world, where hard-core pornography is not banned, is that in our world, there are competitors to the message of hard-core pornography that serve to undercut its practical impact on people's actions. To some degree this is true. There are competitors—for example, what MacKinnon calls "erotica" or sexually explicit materials—that are premised on equality.[60] The problem is that in our world, these competitors tend to be overwhelmed by the multi-billion-dollar pornography industry, which probably is now, at least in the United States, the dominant educator of boys and young men with respect to how to engage in intimate sexual relations.[61]

This suggests that what is important is not whether some message is classified as speech but rather the impact it has on people's lives.[62] In a world where there is a complete reversal of poetic justice, the impact of such a message on people's lives would surely be judged harmful enough to justify a coercive corrective. In our world, in which hard-core pornography depicts a complete reversal of poetic justice with respect to sexual relations, the impact of such a message on people's lives, particularly the lives of women, should similarly be judged harmful enough to justify a coercive corrective.

But why then has a coercive response against hard-core pornography not been more forthcoming, particularly in Western countries? Well, of course, there has been a coercive response in some places; Canada's Supreme Court has recently banned hard-core pornography explicitly on the grounds that it is harmful to women.[63] But most other Western countries have not followed

Canada's lead in this regard. One explanation for this failure to act is the difficulty of separating hard-core pornography, which is arguably harmful to women, from forms of soft-core pornography, which are arguably not harmful to women. But the line here between hard-core and soft-core pornography does not need to be drawn with any high degree of precision. It suffices if the law is used to prosecute the worse cases of hard-core pornography characterized as being sexually explicit, violent, and sexist in order to begin to undercut hard-core pornography's grip on men's psyches.

Yet another explanation of why hard-core pornography has not been banned in more places is more difficult to overcome. It is that far too many people do not see hard-core pornography for what it is. For them hard-core pornography represents either acceptable or even desirable sexual relations between women and men, and so they have basically no problem with its spillover into practice.

In addition, some women may underestimate the harmfulness of hard-core pornography. They may sample hard-core pornography and find that they have little difficulty renouncing the submissive and degraded images of the women that it displays. They may then mistakenly infer from their own reactions to hard-core pornography that men should have little difficulty doing the same.[64]

Here it would be helpful if men were to explain how their reactions to hard-core pornography are typically different from women's. They should explain how hard-core pornography when combined with the pleasures of masturbation can enter their psyches and structure their sexual tastes in ways that can be quite difficult to resist.[65] This happens whenever the sexual images drawn from hard-core pornography impose themselves on men's real-life encounters demanding to be reenacted as the price of sexual pleasure. Men can easily find themselves in a situation where they cannot easily achieve orgasm without somehow incorporating the sexual images of hard-core pornography into their lives, leading them either to impose or to try to impose hard-core pornographic roles on the women who come into their lives, with more or less harmful effects. It is just in this regard that men can testify to the destructive impact hard-core pornography can have on their relations with women, and thereby help demonstrate the necessity for banning it.

In so many contexts, women are in a much better position than men to expose and argue against the harmful effects of sexist practices. Generally, nothing succeeds better at sharpening one's perception of unjust practices or at developing one's argumentative skills to oppose such practices than actually having suffered from them oneself. That is why women's subjection to the injustice of sexist practices makes them the obvious leaders in the fight to rid society of those practices. Nevertheless, there are a number of contexts where men are in a particularly good position to contribute to women's liberation, and one of these is the role they can play in exposing the harmful effects that hard-core pornography can have on their own lives and on the lives of the women with whom they come in contact.[66]

In sum, traditional ethics has failed to apply the public/private distinction in ways that adequately take women's perspectives into account. To properly apply the distinction, we need to acknowledge that family life belongs, in large part, within the public domain, and then we need to go on to specify how the law should regulate and control family life so as to guarantee equal opportunity to both women and men. We also need to acknowledge that the effects of the consumption of hard-core pornography belong not to the private but to the public domain and that the production and sale of hard-core pornography need to be legally prohibited because of their harmful effects, particularly on the lives of women.

The Practical Inadequacy of the Traditional Ideals of a Morally Good Person

In addition to the practical inadequacy of its theories of justice and its public/private distinction, traditional ethics has also failed to properly take women's interests into account when specifying its ideals of a morally good person.

In the Kantian ethics developed by John Rawls, a morally good person is one whose actions conform to the principles which would be unanimously chosen by persons behind an imaginary veil of ignorance.[67] These principles specify the proper distribution of basic liberties, opportunities and economic goods in society, and what rights and duties people have with respect to these social goods. According to Rawls, further specification of a morally good person depends on the particular comprehensive conception of the good that the person endorses, but what he thinks all morally good persons have in common is that they would abide by the principles that would be chosen in his original position.

In utilitarian ethics, a morally good person is one whose actions maximize the net utility or satisfaction of everyone affected by them. But normally in order for a person's action to maximize net utility, a person needs to follow certain rules and practices. Trying to directly determine with respect to each of our actions what would maximize net utility would not only require far more reflection than we are capable of, it would also be counterproductive. So in utilitarian ethics, a morally good person is one who generally follows the best rules and practices for maximizing utility in his or her society, only attempting to directly calculate the utility of the available options when those rules and practices come into conflict.

In Aristotelian ethics, a morally good person is one whose actions, for the most part, further his or her proper development as a human being. For Aristotelians, one's proper development as a human being is further specified as acting in conformity with a set of virtues, the most important of which are prudence, justice, courage, and temperance, and what these virtues require is generally determined by the morally best practices of one's society.

Now while Kantian ethics, utilitarian ethics, and Aristotelian ethics all specify their ideals of a morally good person somewhat differently, from a feminist standpoint, the general problem with them all is that they specify their ideals so abstractly that they fail to deal with the question of whether we should conform to the distinctive gender roles that women and men are socialized into in our society. Thus, when we think stereotypically about men and women in our society, we come up with different lists of desirable and undesirable traits, such as the following:

Men	*Women*
Independent	*Dependent*
Competitive	Cooperative
Aggressive, assertive	Nurturant, caring
Unemotional, stoic, detached	Emotional
Active, *violent*	*Passive,* nonviolent
Unconcerned with appearance	*Concerned with appearance (vain)*
Dominant	*Submissive,* self-effacing
Decisive	*Indecisive*
Seen as subject	Seen as object (of beauty or sexual attraction)
Sloppy	Neat
Sexually active	*Slut or nun*
Reasonable, rational, logical	Intuitive, *illogical*
Protective	In need of protection
Insensitive	Sensitive

If we assume that the traits in *italics* are obviously undesirable ones, then in addition to having quite different stereotypical traits associated with men and women in our society, we also have more undesirable traits on the women's list than on the men's.

How should we think about such lists? Surely they reflect the gender roles and traits which boys and girls, men and women are socialized into in society. In the past, the desirable gender traits stereotypically associated with men were thought to characterize mental health.[68] More recently, these same traits have been used to describe the successful corporate executive.[69] Distinctive gender roles and traits have been used in these ways to favor men over women. Nevertheless, traditional ethics with its relatively abstract specification of its ideals of a morally good person has failed to take up the question of whether or not we should conform to those distinctive gender roles, thereby, through neglect, implicitly endorsing those very gender roles and traits. This has rendered the traditional ideals of a morally good person practically inadequate in a way that is biased against women.

Nor is traditional ethics without resources to deal with the question of gender roles in society. If we want to adequately take into account the interests of women, the appropriate answer to the question of whether we should maintain distinctive gender roles and traits in society is clear. It is that we need to replace these distinctive gender roles and traits with an ideal which makes all truly desirable traits that can be distributed in society equally open to both women and men. More accurately, we need to require that the traits which are truly desirable and distributable in society be equally open to both women and men or, in the case of virtues, be equally expected of both women and men, other things being equal.

To distinguish traits of character that are virtues from those that are merely desirable let us define the class of virtues as those desirable and distributable traits that can be reasonably expected of both women and men. Admittedly, this is a restrictive use of the term "virtue." In normal usage, "virtue" is almost synonymous with "desirable trait."[70] But there is good reason to focus on those desirable traits that can be justifiably inculcated in both women and men, and so for our purposes let us refer to this class of desirable traits as virtues.

So characterized, this ideal represents neither a revolt against so-called feminine virtues and traits nor their exaltation over so-called masculine virtues and traits.[71] This is because the ideal does not view women's liberation as simply the freeing of women from the confines of traditional roles, which makes it possible for them to develop in ways heretofore reserved for men. Nor does the ideal view women's liberation as simply the reevaluation and glorification of so-called feminine activities like housekeeping or mothering or so-called feminine modes of thinking as reflected in an ethic of caring. The first perspective ignores or devalues genuine virtues and desirable traits traditionally associated with women while the second ignores or devalues genuine virtues and desirable traits traditionally associated with men. In contrast, this ideal seeks a broader-based ideal for both women and men that combines virtues and desirable traits traditionally associated with women with virtues and desirable traits traditionally associated with men. For this reason, we can call it the ideal of androgyny, a common ideal for both men (*andro-*) and women (*-gyne*).

This ideal of androgyny should be part of the practical specification of the ideals of a morally good person whether those ideals are Kantian, utilitarian, or Aristotelian. It should be seen as what persons behind an imaginary veil of ignorance, persons whose actions maximize the net utility or satisfaction of everyone affected by them, and persons seeking their proper development as human beings, would all endorse. Accordingly, only when traditional ethics includes the ideal of androgyny within the practical specification of its ideals of a morally good person, will it succeed in being practically adequate in a way that also avoids being biased against women.

It is also important to see that the ideal of androgyny, which must be included in the practical specification of the ideals of a morally good person if traditional ethics is to succeed in being practically adequate, is itself a specification of the ideal of equal opportunity. That is why, when we earlier applied the ideal of equal opportunity to family structures, as required by a practically adequate conception of justice and by a practically adequate application of the public/private distinction, it ruled out the possibility of gendered families. It is also why the various ways we have discussed of helping to create equal opportunity between women and men both inside and outside of family life, such as an effective mix of paid and unpaid parental leave, adequate day care, equitable divorce laws, laws banning hard-core pornography, equal sharing of housekeeping and childrearing, equal pay for equal or comparable work, and prohibiting gender-based advertising directed at children, are also ways of helping to realize the ideal of androgyny. In recent times, Carol Gilligan's work has given rise to the challenge that traditional ethics is biased against women. In this chapter, I have argued that the bias of traditional ethics is manifested by the practical inadequacy of its theories of justice, its public/private distinction, and its ideals of a morally good person. I have further argued that traditional ethics can overcome this bias by applying its theories of justice, its public/private distinction, and its ideals of a morally good person so as to rule out gendered family structures and to implement an ideal of androgyny. This is what is required if traditional ethics is to meet the challenge of feminism and adequately take women's perspectives into account.

4

MULTICULTURALISM

The Western Bias in Traditional Ethics and How to Correct It

The failure of traditional ethics to sufficiently take into account non-Western cultures, especially with respect to the canon of what should be taught, is what gives rise to the multiculturalist challenge that traditional ethics is biased in favor of Western culture. Recent interest in this challenge of multiculturalism to traditional ethics dates from a more general multicultural challenge to the educational canon that provoked a national debate in the United States in the late 1980s and early 1990s.[1] This national debate focused on Stanford University's revision of its Western civilization course that introduced an *optional* eighth-track version of the course in which the required elements of the European canon remained, but were read along with works of Spanish-American, American Indian, and African-American authors.[2] Even these minimal changes, however, were roundly attacked. For example, then secretary of education William Bennett paid a visit to Stanford to criticize the changes.[3] George Will, in his national column, wrote that courses at Stanford should "affirm this fact: America is predominantly a product of the Western tradition and is predominantly good because that tradition is good."[4] William F. Buckley Jr. declared that "from Homer to the nineteenth century no great book has emerged from any non-European source."[5] In agreement with Buckley, Saul Bellow remarked, "When the Zulus have a Tolstoy, we will read him."[6] Such opposition to opening up the educational canon to non-Western sources is particularly striking when one recognizes that over 50 percent of the undergraduate students at Stanford, Berkeley, and UCLA are nonwhite, as are over 30 percent of all U.S. undergraduate students.[7] It is even more striking when one reflects that if current trends continue, a near majority of the U.S. population will be of minority origin by 2040.[8]

Now the multicultural challenge to traditional ethics parallels this more general multicultural challenge to the educational canon. Its central claim is that if Western moral ideals are to be defensible, they must be able to survive a comparative evaluation with other moral ideals, including non-Western ones.[9] So it claims there is no escaping an adequate representation of non-Western moral ideals in the canon of what should be taught.

It might be objected, however, that the justification of our moral ideals is not comparative, but rather grounded in a rationality that is required of each and every human being. To some degree this would be true if the argument offered in chapter 1 were successful, that is, if rationality understood as non-question-beggingness did require us to endorse morality over both egoism and pure altruism. Unfortunately, most contemporary moral philosophers do not think that arguments of this sort can succeed and so they cannot avail themselves of this way of avoiding the need to provide a comparative justification of the moral ideals they endorse—one that includes a comparative evaluation of non-Western moral ideals. Moreover, even if the particular attempt in chapter 1 to show that morality is rationally required were successful, it would still not eliminate the need for a comparative evaluation of moral ideals. This is because the argument, if successful, only succeeds in showing that morality is rationally preferable to egoism or pure altruism. It does not clearly establish which particular form of morality is preferable. To do that, we need a comparable evaluation of alternative moral ideals, and to avoid bias, that evaluation must take into account non-Western moral ideals.

Unfortunately, traditional ethics, by and large, has simply ignored the need for a comparative evaluation of this sort. It has rested content offering a comparative evaluation that is limited to Western moral ideals such as the Aristotelian, utilitarian, and Kantian perspectives discussed in chapter 1. In this way, traditional ethics has shown itself to be biased against non-Western ideals and has thereby failed to provide an adequate justification of its own moral ideals.

It is important to reflect upon what sort of a comparative evaluation is actually needed here. The ethics we are looking for should be able to provide sufficient reasons accessible to all those to whom it applies for abiding by its requirements. So it must be an ethics that is capable of justifying the use of power to enforce its basic requirements. To do that, it must be possible for the ethics to justifiably morally blame those who are coerced for failing to abide by its requirements. If that were not the case, people could justifiably resist such uses of power on the ground that they would lack moral legitimacy.[10] People cannot be morally required to do something if they cannot come to know, and so come to justifiably believe, that they are required to do so. So if an ethics is to be able to justify the use of power to enforce its basic requirements, there must be sufficient reasons accessible to all those to whom it applies for abiding by those requirements. What this means is that the ethics we are seeking must be secular rather than religious in character, because only secular reasons are accessible to everyone; religious reasons are primarily accessible only to the members of the particular religious groups who hold them, and as such they cannot provide the justification that is needed to support the use of power to enforce the basic requirements of morality.

Now it might be objected that at least some religious reasons are accessible to virtually everyone who has been exposed to them. Of course, many people today have not even been exposed to the teachings of the four dominant religions, Christianity, Islam, Buddhism, and Hinduism, and even for those who have, mere exposure, by itself, is not enough to guarantee the kind of accessibility that would justify the use of power against those who fail to abide by their teachings. For that to be the case, exposure must necessarily lead to the idea that it would be unreasonable to reject those teachings as such. In the case of Christian moral teachings, this would mean that it would be unreasonable to reject these teachings as part of a unique Christian salvation history, which has as key events an incarnation, a redemptive death, and a resurrection.

Of course, this is not to deny that some religious teachings can be given a justification that is independent of their religious origin (e.g., the story of the good Samaritan[11])—a justification that is accessible to virtually everyone exposed to these teachings on the grounds that virtually everyone so exposed would understand that it would be unreasonable to reject them, so justified. But the objection we are considering does not address the possibility of justifying religious moral teachings in this way. Rather, it claims that religious moral teachings are justified because *as such* they are accessible to virtually everyone exposed to them with the consequence that it would be unreasonable for virtually anyone so exposed to reject them.

But is this the case? Surely many Christian moral teachings, for example, are understandable to both Christians and non-Christians alike, but the sense of "accessible" we have been using implies more than this. It implies that persons can be morally blamed for failing to abide by accessible requirements because they can come to understand that these requirements apply to them and that it would be unreasonable for them to fail to abide by them. So understood, it would seem that, for example, Christian moral teachings *as such* are not accessible to everyone exposed to them. Too many non-Christians, who seem otherwise moral, do not recognize the authority of Christian moral teachings as such, even though they may grant that some of these teachings have an independent justification.

Accordingly, we are looking for an ethics that is secular in character and thus one that can provide sufficient reasons accessible to all those to whom it applies for abiding by its requirements. It must be an ethics that is capable of justifying the use of power to enforce its basic requirements. Specifying it will require a wide-ranging comparative evaluation of both Western and non-Western moral ideals. That is why the failure of traditional ethics to take into account non-Western moral ideals is so important. It has undercut the possibility of providing a defensible ethics for our time. Accordingly, we must do what we can to correct for this failure of traditional ethics.

There are various ways that non-Western cultures can contribute to fashioning a defensible ethics for our time. In this chapter, I want to consider three of these ways. First, non-Western moral ideals can help to significantly correct and interpret our Western moral ideals. Second, non-Western cultures can help us recognize important obligations that flow from our moral ideals which we either did not recognize or fully recognize before. Third, non-Western cultures can help us to know how best to apply our own moral ideals, especially cross-culturally.[12]

Correcting and Interpreting Traditional Ethics

Using American Indian Culture

Traditional ethics has focused on the debate between Aristotelian, utilitarian, and Kantian views. In chapter 1, I argued that in this debate there are good reasons for favoring a Kantian view over a utilitarian or an Aristotelian view. But however this debate is resolved, it still may be that traditional ethics is not demanding enough, because it has not adequately faced the question of who is to count in ways that at least some non-Western moral perspectives have done.[13] In traditional ethics, it is assumed that only human beings have the moral status of persons. By contrast, many if not all American Indian tribes regard animals, plants, and assorted other natural things as having the moral status of persons with whom it is possible to enter into complex social intercourse requiring mutual respect.[14] The type of respect required is illustrated by the following account of how a Sioux elder advised his son to hunt the four-legged animals of the forest:

> (S)hoot your four-legged brother in the hind area, slowing it down but not killing it. Then, take the four-legged's head in your hands, and look into his eyes. The eyes are where all the suffering is. Look into your brother's eyes and feel his pain. Then, take your knife and cut the four-legged under his chin, here, on his neck, so that he dies quickly. And as you do, ask your brother, the four-legged, for forgiveness for what you do. Offer also a prayer of thanks to your four-legged kin for offering his body to you just now, when you need food to eat and clothing to wear. And promise the four-

legged that you will put yourself back into the earth when you die, to become the nourishment of the earth, and for the sister flowers, and for the brother deer. It is appropriate that you should offer this blessing for the four-legged and, in due time, reciprocate in turn with your body in this way, as the four-legged gives life to you for your survival.[15]

Wooden Leg, a Cheyenne, provides a similar account:

The old Indian teaching was that it is wrong to tear loose from its place on the earth anything that may be growing there. It may be cut off, but it should not be uprooted. The trees and the grass have spirits. Whenever one of such growths may be destroyed by some good Indian, his act is done in sadness and with a prayer for forgiveness because of necessities.[16]

Moreover, this respect for nonhuman nature shared by American Indians is based on a perceived identity with other living things. According to Luther Standing Bear, a Sioux chief,

We are the soil and the soil is us. We love the birds and beasts that grew with us on this soil. They drank the same water as we did and breathed the same air. We are all one in nature. Believing so, there was in our hearts a great peace and a welling kindness for all living growing things.[17]

Jorge Valadez has also pointed out that for the Mayans of Central America, nature is not something to be mastered and controlled for human purposes.[18] The Mayans saw themselves not as standing against nature but rather as an integral part of it. Similarly, Moshoeshoe II argues that within indigenous African culture there is a deep respect for the natural environment.[19] Arguably, it is this respect for nonhuman nature that has enabled people in non-Western cultures to live in their natural environment with greater harmony than we in Western culture are presently doing.[20]

Is there, then, something that we in Western culture can learn from these non-Western cultures? At the very least, an appreciation for these cultures should lead us to consider whether we have legitimate grounds for failing to constrain our own interests for the sake of nonhuman nature. In Western culture, people tend to think of themselves as radically separate from and superior to non-human nature, so as to allow for domination over it. To justify this perspective, people in Western culture often appeal to the creation story in Genesis in which God tells humans to

> be fruitful and multiply, and fill the earth and subdue it. Have do-minion over the fish of the sea, the birds of the air, cattle, and all the animals that crawl on the earth. (Genesis 1:28)

As we noted before, one interpretation of this directive is that hu-mans are required or permitted to dominate nonhuman nature, that is, to use animals and plants for whatever purpose we wish, giv-ing no independent weight at all to the interests of animals and plants. Another interpretation, however, understands dominion, not as domination, but as a caring stewardship toward nonhuman nature, which imposes limits on the ways that we can use animals and plants in pursuit of our own purposes, thereby making it pos-sible for other living things to flourish.

Obviously, this second interpretation accords better with the perspective found in American Indian and other non-Western cul-tures. However, it is the first interpretation that is most widely accepted throughout Western culture. Given these conflicting in-terpretations of the Genesis story, it is clear that an appeal to the Bible is not going to be decisive in determining how anyone should treat nonhuman nature. Accordingly, we need to determine whether reason alone can provide any compelling grounds for thinking that we are superior to nonhuman nature in ways that would justify our domination of it. In chapter 2, I took up this question and argued on the basis of reason alone that there are no grounds for thinking that we are superior to nonhuman nature in ways that would justify our domination of it. If this argument is correct, then those of us within Western culture can learn an im-portant lesson from American Indian and other non-Western cul-tures. It is that the intrinsic value of nonhuman species places a significant constraint on how we pursue our own interests, a constraint that requires us to reinterpret our basic human rights so as to rule out the domination of nonhuman nature.

Using Confucius

A central problem in traditional ethics is how to get people to strongly identify themselves with particular groups, such as families, communities, or nations, so that they will be more willing to act for the good of those groups, while at the same time getting them to think critically about the groups to which they belong so as to avoid doing considerable harm to themselves and others when pursuing the interests of those groups. To accomplish this task, we do well to consult the work of the Chinese philosopher Confucius.

Kung Fu-tzu or Confucius, his Latinized name, lived from c. 551 to 479 B.C., about 150 years before Plato. He was not known to the Western world until the late sixteenth century when Jesuit missionaries in an effort to convert Chinese rulers steeped themselves in ancient Confucian literature and were overwhelmed by what they found.[21]

Soon reports made their way back to Europe. Leibniz wrote that the Chinese surpassed Europeans in practical philosophy and recommended that Chinese missionaries be sent to Europe, and Voltaire declared that in morality Europeans "ought to become disciples" of the Chinese.[22] Christian Wolff said of the Chinese that "in the art of governing, this nation has ever surpassed all others without exception."[23] Confucius became known as the patron saint of the Enlightenment.[24]

Confucius was remarkably successful as a teacher. The *Analects* is a collection of his sayings, probably compiled by his students. Of the twenty-two students mentioned in the *Analects,* nine attained important government posts and a tenth turned one down. Moreover, his impact was far-reaching. For 2,500 years, he was "the Master" to all of China, and his influence continued even after the Communist revolution and is more in evidence today.

Like Plato and later Aristotle, Confucius advocates a virtue ethics, but the list of virtues that he advocates is longer than the list of virtues advocated by Plato and different in certain respects from the list advocated by Aristotle. One distinctive feature of Confucius's ethics is his stress on filial obligation. For Plato, the just individual is modeled on the just state, but for Confucius, the state should be thought of as the family writ large. Confucius also advocates meritocracy, various forms of which were incorporated into Chinese society. The British civil service system was actually modeled on the system found in China, and the civil service system in the United States was in turn modeled after the British system, and so ultimately on the Chinese system as well. One also finds in Confucius negative versions of the golden rule: "What you do not want done to yourself, do not do to others." No wonder then that one of the Jesuit missionaries, impressed by Confucius's views, affirmed that if Confucius had lived in the seventeenth century, "he would have been the first to become a Christian."

If we look to Confucius for help in understanding how we can get people to strongly identify themselves with particular groups and, at the same time, think critically about the groups to which they belong, we find two central concepts: *jen* and *li*.[25] *Jen* refers, most of the time, to the highest ethical ideal, including such qualities as concern for the well-being of others, filial piety, respect for elders, and the ability to endure adverse circumstances. *Li* originally referred to the rites of sacrifice to spirits and ancestors, but eventually it came to refer to all traditional and customary norms governing the relationship between people. In a number of places in the *Analects*, Confucius remarks on the intimate connection between *jen* and *li*. When asked about *jen* (in 12:1) Confucius says, "To return to the practice of *li* through the subduing of self constitutes *jen*." In 1:2, Confucius describes filial piety as the essential starting point for cultivating *jen*, and in another place filial piety is explained in terms of the observance of *li*.

These passages could lead us to interpret Confucius as an extreme traditionalist who advocated an uncritical acceptance of traditional and customary norms, but from what Confucius says elsewhere it is clear that he envisions *jen* as having a critical function with respect to *li*. For example, in 9:3 he says,

A ceremonial cap of linen is what is prescribed by *li*. Today black silk is used instead. This is more frugal and I follow the majority. To prostrate oneself before ascending the steps (to enter the presence of the prince) is what is prescribed by *li*. Today one does so after having ascended them. This is casual and, though going against the majority, I follow the practice of doing so before ascending.

In this passage, Confucius is clearly evaluating two conflicts between current common practices and older rules, favoring the common practice in one case and an older rule in the other, in terms of their appropriateness for securing *jen*.

But how do we know when to abide by common or customary practices and when to depart from them? Sometimes this can be quite difficult to determine. In 13:18, the governor of She informs Confucius, "In our village there is one who may be styled upright in his conduct. When his father stole a sheep, he gave evidence against him." Confucius replies, "In our village, those who are upright are quite different. Fathers conceal the misconduct of their sons and sons conceal the misconduct of their fathers." But surely there are limits to the degree to which one should conceal the misconduct of one's relatives. It was surely appropriate for David Kaczynski to turn in his brother, the Unabomber, who over seventeen years had planted sixteen bombs at various locations in the United States, killing three and injuring twenty-nine people.[26]

Consider another case. In her book *Woman Warrior*, Maxine Hong Kingston retells a traditional Chinese ballad of a young woman who takes the place of her aged father when he is called into the army.[27] Kingston juxtaposes the "perfect filiality" of the woman warrior with her own inability to win from her family or community any appreciation for her worldly achievements. She stresses how women's triumphs are often achieved in the face of familial or societal opposition. What these examples show is that it is not always easy to know when we should abide by the common or customary practices of our society and when we should depart from them. Clearly, much depends on what alternatives are actually available to us in the historical circumstances in which we find ourselves. After all, "ought" does imply "can," and so we cannot be morally required to do what it would be unreasonable to expect us to do. What this discussion of Confucian ethics shows, however, is that sometimes we need to rebel against common or customary practices, and that sometimes we need to do so for the sake of traditional values themselves.

New Obligations for Traditional Ethics

In "Perversions of Justice: A Native-American Examination of the Doctrine of U.S. Rights to Occupancy in North America," Native American activist Ward Churchill argues that the United States does not now possess, nor has it ever possessed, a legitimate right to occupancy in at least half the territory it claims as its own on this continent.[28] He further argues that Iraq had a far better claim to Kuwait (its nineteenth province, separated from it by the British after World War I) than the U.S. government has to virtually any part of North America.[29] Certainly, this is not a widely held perspective in Western societies. It certainly is not the perspective that is endorsed in the textbooks approved by the conservative state boards in Texas and California, which because of the size of their markets set the standard for textbook publishers across the United States.[30] Nevertheless, if traditional ethics is to avoid bias against non-Western ideals, it must come to terms with Churchill's Native American perspective, assessing what implications it has, if any, for our obligations to Native Americans today. To do that, we need to take another look at the conquest of the American Indians by the Europeans who came to the New World.

Recent estimates put the Indian population of North and South America before the arrival of Columbus at around 100 million, with about 15 million of these Indians living north of the Rio Grande. For comparison, the population of Europe at that time was about 70 million, the population of Russia about 18 million and Africa about 72 million.[31] When Columbus arrived in the Caribbean Islands, he was greeted by a people who called themselves the Taino. Columbus describes them in a letter to the king and queen of Spain:

> So tractable, so peaceful are these people that I swear to your Majesties there is not in the world a better nation. They love their neighbors as themselves, and their discourse is sweet and gentle,

and accompanied with a smile; and though it is true they are naked, yet their manners are decorous and praiseworthy.[32]

In 1492, about 8 million loosely organized Taino inhabited the island which Columbus called Hispaniola and which constitutes present-day Haiti and the Dominican Republic. By 1508, the population of Hispaniola was less than 100,000. By 1518, it numbered less than 20,000. Scholars agree that by 1535, for all practical purposes, the native population of Hispaniola was extinct.[33]

What happened to the Taino of Hispaniola? To some degree they were wiped out by the diseases that the Spaniards had brought with them, but that was only part of the story.[34] The other part was that the Spaniards wanted gold; they wanted all the gold the Taino could provide, and they wanted it quickly. To secure it, the Spaniards chose to terrorize the Indians into providing them with gold. According to Las Casas, the Spaniards

> slew many Indians by hanging, burning, and being torn to pieces by savage dogs, also by cutting the hands and feet and heads and tongues, and for no other reason than to spread terror and induce the Indians to give them gold.[35]

In pursuit of this policy, the Spaniards

> attacked the towns and spared neither the children nor the aged nor pregnant women nor women in childbed, not only stabbing them and dismembering them but cutting them to pieces as if dealing with sheep in the slaughter house. They laid bets as to who, with one stroke of the sword, could split a man in two or could cut off his head or spill his entrails with a single stroke of the pike. They took infants from their mothers' breasts, snatching them by the legs and pitching them headfirst against the crags or snatching them by the arms and throwing them into rivers, roaring with laughter. . . . They made some low wide gallows on which the hanged victim's feet almost touched the ground, stringing up their victims in lots of thirteen, in memory of Our Redeemer and His twelve Apostles, then set burning wood at their feet and thus burned them alive.[36]

Every Indian on the island of Hispaniola who was not a child was ordered to deliver to the Spanish a certain amount of precious ore every three months. Indians who delivered the ore were given a token to wear around their necks as proof that the tribute had been paid. The quotas were so high, however, that the Indians could not meet them and maintain their food production. Consequently, many died of starvation or in their weakened condition perished more easily from the new diseases brought by the Spaniards.[37] In this way, the Spaniards not only depopulated Hispaniola but also the other islands of the Caribbean such San Juan, Jamaica, and Cuba.

In central Mexico, it is estimated that the population was about 25 million in 1519 when Hernando Cortes arrived. By 1595, it had been reduced by 95 percent to 1,300,000.[38] Unlike the Caribbean people whom the Spaniards first encountered, however, the inhabitants of Mexico had a good deal of experience with warfare. Even so, two factors enabled the Spaniards to dominate. First, Cortes was able to enlist rival Indian nations in his campaign against the Aztecs and their ruler, Montezuma. Thus, Cortes refers to 150,000 warriors accompanying his band of less than a thousand Spanish soldiers as they marched on the Aztecs' capital, Tenochtitlán. Second, the Aztecs believed in declaring war and fighting it fairly; they would go so far as to send food and weapons to an enemy before attacking in order to have a worthy adversary. Consequently, they did not believe that Cortes, who professed his peaceful intentions, would actually attack them once his forces were within the city.[39]

With the Aztecs defeated, the Spaniards continued their search for gold. Las Casas recounts the story of a local ruler who had given the Spaniards, either of his own accord or impelled by fear, gold worth nine thousand castellanos.[40] Not content with this amount, the Spaniards had the ruler bound to a stake in a sitting position with his legs extended, and set a fire to burn the soles of his feet, demanding more gold. The ruler sent to his house for more gold, and a servant brought back three thousand castellanos worth. Not content with this, they demanded more gold. And, either because there was no more or else because the ruler was unwilling to give more, he continued to be tortured until the bone marrow came out of the soles of his feet and he died. Las Casas comments on this incident, "Such things were done to the Indians countless times, always with the aim of getting as much gold as possible from them."[41]

So wherever the Spaniards went, they continued their policy of terror against the Indians. Las Casas recounts, "The Spaniards cut their faces from the nose and lips down to the chin and sent them in this lamentable condition, streaming with blood, to carry the news of the miraculous things being done by the Spaniards. . . . [On one occasion,] seventy pairs of hands were cut off."[42]

With central Mexico wasted, the Spaniards moved south. In Peru and Chile, the home of the Incas, there were at least 9 million inhabitants before Francisco Pizarro arrived in 1533. By the turn of the century, their number had been reduced to about 500,000. Here the Spaniards, after initially dispossessing the Incas of their gold and silver, enslaved them to work either in silver mines high in the Andes Mountains or on coca plantations in the coastal lowlands. Taking the supply of Indians to be inexhaustible, the Spaniards did little to maintain the Indians laboring in the mines or on the plantations, so that their life expectancy in each case was not much more than three or four months—about the same as the life expectancy of a slave laborer at Auschwitz in the 1940s.[43]

By the end of the sixteenth century, scholars estimate that about 200,000 Spaniards had moved to the Indies, to Mexico, and to Central and South America. Scholars also estimate that by that time between 60 million and 80 million natives from those lands were dead.[44]

While fewer Indians lived north of the Rio Grande, the prevailing British, and later American, attitude to these Indians was, if anything, harsher than that of the Spaniards. What the British, and later the Americans, wanted was land—the very same land that the Indians occupied. As Edward Waterhouse, a Jamestown settler, put it, "We shall enjoy their cultivated places . . . [and] their cleared grounds in all their villages (which are situated in the fruitfullest places of the land) shall be inhabited by us."[45] Specifically, the goal was either to push the Indians westward or to exterminate them.

This goal was clearly endorsed at the highest levels of society. In 1779, George Washington ordered Major General John Sullivan to attack the Iroquois and "lay waste all the settlements around . . . that the country may not be merely overrun but destroyed," urging the general not to "listen to any overture of peace before the total ruin of their settlements is effected."[46] Surviving Indians referred to Washington by the nickname "Town Destroyer" because under his direct orders twenty-eight out of thirty Seneca towns from Lake Erie to the Mohawk River and *all* the towns and villages of the Mohawk, the Onondaga, and the Cayuga were totally obliterated. As one surviving Iroquois told Washington to his face in 1792, "To this day, when that name is heard, our women look behind them and turn pale, and our children cling close to the necks of their mother."[47]

This goal of removal or extermination was also shared by Adams, Monroe, and Jefferson.[48] For example, Jefferson instructed his Secretary of State in 1807 that any Indians who resisted American expansion must be met with "the hatchet." "And . . . if ever we are constrained to lift the hatchet against any tribe," he wrote, "we will never lay it down till that tribe is exterminated, or driven beyond the Mississippi, " adding that "in war, they will kill some of us, [but] we shall destroy all of them."[49] To achieve this destruction, the British, and later the Americans, were not averse to distributing smallpox-infected blankets among the Indians as Sir Jeffrey Amherst did against Pontiac's confederation in 1763 and as the U.S. Army did to decimate the Mandans along the Missouri River in present-day South Dakota in 1836.[50]

In 1828 Andrew Jackson, who had once written that "the whole Cherokee nation ought to be scourged," was elected president of the United States. Jackson supported the state of Georgia's attempt to appropriate a large portion of Cherokee land.[51] When the U.S. Supreme Court ruled against Jackson and Georgia, Jackson had a treaty drawn up ceding the Cherokee lands to the American government in exchange for money and some land in the Indian Territory of Oklahoma. With the most influential leader of the Cherokees imprisoned and their tribal printing press shut down by the government, a treaty was negotiated with certain "cooperative"

Cherokees. Yet even the American military officer who was to register the tribe's members for removal protested that this treaty was

> no treaty at all, because [it was] not sanctioned by the great body of the Cherokee and [it was] made without their participation or assent. I solemnly declare to you that upon its reference to the Cherokee people it would be instantly rejected by nine-tenths of them, and I believe by nineteen-twentieths of them.[52]

With this treaty signed, the members of the Cherokee nation were force-marched overland to the Indian Territory, intentionally passing through areas where it was known that cholera and other epidemic diseases were raging. Thus, of the seventeen thousand who began the march, called by the Indians the Trail of Tears, only nine thousand arrived in Oklahoma.

Actually, in the West itself, extermination of the Indians, rather than relocation, seemed to be the preferred policy. For example, Colonel John Chivington, who led seven hundred armed soldiers in a massacre of mostly women and children at Sand Creek in Colorado in 1864, announced earlier that he wanted his troops to "kill and scalp all, little and big," noting that "nits make lice."[53] And in 1867 when Tosawi, a chief of the Comanches, introduced himself to General Philip Sheridan with "Tosawi, good Indian," Sheridan responded with his often quoted remark, "The only good Indians I ever saw were dead."[54]

There is little doubt that Chivington's and Sheridan's views were widely shared. For example, Oliver Wendell Holmes claimed that Indians were nothing more than a "half-filled outline of humanity" whose "extermination" was the necessary "solution to the problem of [their] relation to the white race."[55] Similarly, William Dean Howells took "patriotic pride" in advocating "the extermination of the red savages of the plains."[56] And Theodore Roosevelt maintained that the extermination of the American Indians and the expropriation of their lands "was as ultimately beneficial as it was inevitable."[57] In Texas, an official bounty on native scalps—*any* native scalps—was maintained well into the 1870s.[58]

In 1890, the U.S. government declared the period of conquest called "Indian Wars" to be officially over. At that time, it also determined that only 248,253 Indians remained alive within its borders, with another 122,585 residing in Canada.[59] This represented a 98 percent decline from pre-Columbian times.

In the final stages of the European conquest, American Indian children were taken from their parents at early ages, sent to boarding schools, and educated in "white" ways.[60] As the director of one of these schools put it, the goal was to "kill the Indian . . . and save the man." In 1887, more than fourteen thousand Indian children were enrolled in such boarding schools. When the students eventually returned to their reservations, they were virtual strangers, unable to speak their own language or understand the ways of their people.[61]

Nor were these atrocities in any way compensated for by way of providing American Indians with good opportunities to develop themselves and become respectable members of society. Currently, the poverty rate on American Indian reservations in the United States is almost four times the national average, and on some reservations, such as Pine Ridge in South Dakota and Tohomo O'Odham in Arizona (where more than 60 percent of homes are without adequate plumbing, compared with 2 percent for the nation at large), the poverty rate is nearly five times the national average.[62] As late as 1969, the average life expectancy for an Indian was forty-four years, compared to sixty-five for a non-Indian.[63] The suicide rate among young Indians aged fifteen to twenty-four years is also around 200 percent above the national average for the same age group, and the rate for alcohol-caused mortality is more than 900 percent higher than the national average. The destitution and ill health that prevails on many reservations today is similar to conditions in the third world.[64] American Indians today suffer not only from alienation but from extreme social and economic injustice as well.

If we compare the conquest of the American Indians with the Holocaust in Europe, two aspects stand out. First, a far greater number of American Indians lost their lives during the European conquest of North and South America than did Jews during the Holocaust: 74 million to 94 million American Indians compared to 6 million Jews. Second, not only were many Indian peoples, like the Jews, threatened with extinction, but many Indian peoples were actually driven into extinction; for example, in the state of Texas alone, the once populous Karankawa, Akokisa, Bidui, Tejas, and Coahuilans are now all extinct.[65]

There is also an interesting historical connection between the two evils. The conquest of the American Indians began first, but it, in turn, was affected by events in Spain. In 1492, as Columbus set sail for the New World, Jews, ultimately 120,000 to 150,000, were being deported from Spain, and on subsequent trips Columbus brought with him heavily armed and armored infantry and cavalry fresh from their victory over the Moors in Granada.[66] The Spaniards were ready to conquer the New World, and conquer it they did by massacring, enslaving, and decimating all the groups of Indians with whom they came in contact.

Subsequently, however, in the twentieth century, the treatment of the American Indians was used by Nazi leaders to justify inflicting the Holocaust on the Jews. According to Hitler, "Neither Spain nor Britain should be models of German expansion, but the Nordics of North America, who had ruthlessly pushed aside an inferior race to win for themselves soil and territory for the future."[67] Similarly, Heinrich Himmler explained to a confidant that he knew that the Final Solution would mean much suffering for the Jews. But he pointed to what the Americans had done earlier, which was to exterminate the Indians—who only wanted to go on living in their native land—in the most abominable way.[68] Putting the comparison somewhat differently, Ward Churchill wrote in protest of the naming of a building at the University of Colorado at Boulder after Indian-killer-turned-successful-entrepreneur David Nichols:

[When] Germany lost, the crimes of its leaders—both military and civilian—brought out what they were. Their names are now all but universally reviled; no buildings named to commemorate their positive contributions to civilization stand on German campuses. The difference here is that, unlike Germany, the United States won its war of conquest and extermination. If you were ever inclined to wonder what it would be like to live in the Ukraine fifty or a hundred years after a nazi victory, all you need do is look around. You are living it right here, right now. That is why Nichols's name is affixed to a building at the University of Colorado, and the names of men like him are affixed to buildings, streets and parks in thousands of other places around this country today.[69]

Thus, Churchill contrasts the different ways that the Holocaust and the conquest of the American Indians are viewed today, suggesting at the same time how they should be viewed.

So what should be the response of traditional ethics to the conquest of the American Indians—what has been called the American Holocaust?[70] What implications do these past events have for our obligations to American Indians today? Should the United States give a sizable chunk of its land back to the American Indians in view of its history of past injustices? That is exactly what Ward Churchill argues should be done. He notes that the United States entered into and ratified over 370 separate treaties with various nations of American Indians over the first ninety years of its existence.[71] Of course, a number of these ratified treaties were fraudulent or coerced. Sometimes, the United States appointed its own preferred Indian "leaders" to represent their tribes in negotiating the treaties. In at least one case—the treaty of Fort Wise—the U.S. negotiators appear to have forged the signatures of various Cheyenne and Arapaho leaders. There are also about four hundred other treaties that were never ratified by the U.S. Senate and so were never legally binding, but upon which the United States now claims legal title to appreciable portions of North America. Yet even if we assume, just for the sake of argument, that all these treaties are legally and morally binding—something we know is not the case—it still turns out, according to the federal government's own study, that the United States has no legal basis whatsoever—no treaty, no agreement, not even an arbitrary act of Congress—to fully one-third of the area within the lower forty-eight states (the legal claims to Alaska and Hawaii are even more tenuous). At the same time, reserved areas still nominally possessed by Indians represent only 2.5 percent of this same area.

Churchill points out that since the federal and state governments together still own between 45 and 47 percent of the continental

United States, it is possible to restore to American Indian nations 30 percent of the continental landmass, thus restoring to them roughly the percentage of land to which the United States itself admits it has no clear legal title, without evicting any non-Indian homeowners from their land.

Churchill goes on to propose a more specific plan for how this is to be done. Drawing on the work of Frank and Deborah Popper at Rutgers University, he notes that there are 110 counties within the Great Plains region, a quarter of all the counties within the western portions of the states of North and South Dakota, Nebraska, Kansas, Oklahoma, and Texas, as well as eastern Montana, Wyoming, Colorado, and New Mexico that have been fiscally insolvent since the time they were taken away from Indian nations more than a century ago. This is an area of about 140,000 square miles inhabited by a widely dispersed non-Indian population of around 400,000. Without continual federal subsidies, none of these counties would be viable.

What the Poppers proposed is that the government cut its perpetual losses and buy back the individual holdings within these counties, giving the land back to American Indian nations as a Buffalo Commons. Churchill goes further. He notes that there are another one hundred or so counties adjoining the "perpetual red ink" counties which are economically marginal, and suggests that these counties along with national grasslands in Wyoming and national forest and parklands in the Black Hills could be added to the Buffalo Commons. He also suggests that this commons could be extended westward to include Indian reservations and other sparsely populated and economically insolvent regions until it constitutes roughly one-third of the continental United States. It could then be recognized as a sort of North American Union of Indigenous Nations.

So what are we to think of Churchill's plan for restoring Indian lands? If traditional ethics is to adequately take into account the conquest of the American Indians would it not have to recognize an obligation to restore Indian lands, and would that not lead to endorsing either a proposal for a Buffalo Commons or a North American Union of Indigenous Nations? If this would not be required, what would be required? A substantial outlay of economic resources to lift every American Indian out of poverty? Greater authority to open casinos and other tax-free businesses? Whatever is specifically required in order for traditional ethics to adequately take into account an American Indian perspective, it will surely involve recognizing obligations to American Indians that we have not recognized or fully recognized before.

Applying Traditional Ethics Cross-Culturally

Yet even when traditional ethics does not need to be corrected or reinterpreted in light of non-Western ideals, or when knowledge of non-Western cultures is not needed to recognize obligations that we either did not recognize or fully recognize before, it still is the case that knowledge of non-Western cultures is required to apply traditional ethics properly. Failing to consider the relevant local culture or cultures when applying traditional ethics can lead to disastrous results. A well-known example of this sort of failure is the U.S. involvement in Vietnam.

The U.S. involvement in Vietnam began as support for France's efforts to retake its former colony at the end of World War II. But before this support began in earnest, Ho Chi Minh, the leader of the Viet Minh (the Vietnamese Independence Brotherhood League), seized power in Hanoi after the surrender of the Japanese, and with American Office of Strategic Services (OSS) officers in attendance and a Vietnamese band playing "The Star Spangled Banner," proclaimed the independent Republic of Vietnam on September 2, 1945, before a crowd of 500,000 assembled in Ba Dinh Square.[72] Ho's declaration, echoing the famous phrases and the political ideals of the American Declaration of Independence, read as follows:

> All men are created equal. They are endowed by their Creator with certain unalienable rights, among these are Life, Liberty and the Pursuit of Happiness. . . . These are undeniable Truths.
> Nevertheless, for more than eighty years, the French imperialists, abusing the standard of Liberty, Equality and Fraternity, have

violated our Fatherland and oppressed our fellow citizens. Their acts are the opposite of the ideals of humanity and justice.

In the field of politics, they deprived us of all liberties. They have enforced inhuman laws; . . . they have built more prisons than schools. They have mercilessly slain our patriots; they have drowned our uprisings in rivers of blood.

We are convinced that the Allies who recognized the principle of equality of all the peoples at the Conferences of Teheran and San Francisco cannot but recognize the independence of Vietnam. Vietnam has the right to be a free and independent country; and in fact is so already.[73]

A few days before this event, Bao Dai, who had been the puppet emperor of Vietnam during the Japanese occupation, abdicated to the representatives of Ho Chi Minh at the imperial palace at Hue.[74]

From 1943 on, the Viet Minh had been helping American OSS forces rescue downed pilots and escaped prisoners, participating in sabotage missions, and providing better information on Japanese troop movements than the French could provide. American OSS forces in turn provided arms and support to the Viet Minh.[75] All that changed, however, as the U.S. government began to support and finance the return of French colonial forces to Vietnam. Eventually, by the time of France's decisive defeat at Dien Bien Phu in 1954, the United States was shouldering 80 percent of the French war costs.[76]

Unfortunately, the decision to help France retake Vietnam was made with little knowledge of Vietnamese history and culture or the background and character of Ho Chi Minh and the Viet Minh. For example, Franklin Roosevelt once commented that the Vietnamese were a people of "small stature and not warlike."[77] He and other American leaders were unaware of Vietnam's thousand-year struggle against the Chinese and Mongols and its defeat of the fearsome Genghis Khan, of the Trung sisters, and other legendary heroes, nor did they know about the Vietnamese generals who, centuries before Mao Tse-tung, pioneered the art of guerrilla warfare.[78]

Vietnamese recorded history began in 207 B.C.. On that date, Trieu Da, a Chinese warlord, declared himself ruler of a large area encompassing southern China and Vietnam, as far south as present-day Danang. The informal name of this region was "Nam Viet" meaning "land of the southern Viets." Trieu Da ruled his Vietnamese domains indirectly, leaving Viet feudal lords in charge of local affairs. In 111 B.C., Wu-ti, the great Han emperor, conquered Nam Viet. It became a province within the Chinese empire, and for the next thousand years, the northern half of present-day Vietnam was controlled by the Chinese. During this long period of colonial rule, while the Vietnamese adopted many features of Chinese culture, they continued to resist Chinese political domination and economic exploitation. An uprising, long celebrated in Vietnamese history, led by two women, Trung Trac and her sister, Trung Nhi, occurred in A.D. 39. The Trung sisters led an army that overwhelmed the Chinese garrisons stationed on Vietnamese soil and promptly proclaimed themselves the rulers of an independent Viet kingdom. Their rule, however, was short-lived because the emperor sent a strong army that restored Chinese rule in A.D. 43. From the sixth to the tenth century, there were numerous rebellions against the Chinese masters, but they were all suppressed. But after the T'ang dynasty in China fell in 907, a series of uprisings in Vietnam eventually ended Chinese rule. The crucial battle occurred in 939. During that year, a Vietnamese army led by Ngo Quyen confronted a far larger Chinese invasion force, led by the heir to the Chinese throne, along a stretch of the Bach Dang River in the vicinity of present-day Haiphong. Ngo, knowing his forces were outmatched, resorted to a clever stratagem to defeat the more powerful Chinese. He had his soldiers drive iron-tipped stakes into the riverbed so that at high tide the stakes would lie just below the water's surface, hidden from view. With a small flotilla Ngo first attacked the four-hundred-craft Chinese fleet and then ordered his force to feign retreat. The Chinese, sensing victory, pressed after Ngo's retreating ships, passing over the undetected stakes. As the tide began to ebb, Ngo ordered his ships to wheel around just as the Chinese ships were beginning to be impaled on the iron-tipped stakes. With their ships immobilized and sinking, the Vietnamese were able to slaughter the Chinese forces. The imperial heir was taken prisoner and later beheaded. This battle is commemorated as the beginning of Vietnamese national independence.[79]

It had taken the Vietnamese a millennium to win their independence from China in 938. During the next near millennium, until the arrival of the French in the 1850s, every new dynasty that came to power in China invaded Vietnam. These wars with China helped to make central to Vietnamese military thought the idea that an ostensibly weaker force, properly handled, can defeat a stronger one. This idea is hardly new, but the Vietnamese did much to refine it. Vietnamese military teaching emphasized that a more powerful enemy had to be worn down by protracted warfare. Hit-and-run tactics, delaying actions, ambush and harassment by guerrilla bands were to be employed. Finally, when the enemy was sufficiently drained and demoralized, he was to be finished off by a sudden offensive delivered with maximum surprise and deception. The most famous of the early Vietnamese generals, Tran Hung Dao, used this strategy to destroy the Mongols, who burst out of the Gobi Desert to terrorize the world from Korea to Hungary and to subdue China under Genghis Khan and Kublai Khan when they invaded Vietnam in 1284 and again in 1287. A manual on the art of protracted war written by Tran Hung Dao became a classic of Vietnamese military science. Le Loi employed similar tactics to defeat the Ming dynasty generals when they invaded nearly 150 years later.[80]

Three and a half centuries later, these lessons of warfare were still not lost. In 1789, Nguyen Hue, who later ruled under the imperial name Quang Trung, advanced up the central coast into the Red River delta by a series of forced marches. He caught unawares and shattered a much larger invading Manchu army encamped on the outskirts of Hanoi. Violating the sanctity of Tet, the lunar New Year holiday, he attacked at midnight on the fifth day of the holiday while the Manchus were sleeping off the effects of food and wine from the day's celebration. His victory was subsequently remembered on the fifth day of every Tet as the finest single feat of arms in Vietnamese history.[81]

The Vietnamese ideal was the intellectual and man of action who was also a great soldier. The same held true for women. The Trung sisters drowned themselves in A.D. 43 rather than submit after their rebel army had been defeated by the Chinese. As Le Loi, who defeated the Chinese in a nine-year war in the fifteenth century, put it: "We have been weak and we have been strong, but at no time have we lacked heroes."[82]

Unfortunately, the military and cultural history of Vietnam was unknown to those decision makers who initially committed the United States to supporting the French effort to retake their former colony, and presumably unknown as well to those decision makers who later committed the United States to a full-scale military involvement. There was even a failure to appreciate the background and character of Ho Chi Minh and other Viet Minh leaders when these critical decisions were made.

Ho Chi Minh was born in 1890 in Nghe An, a coastal province in central Vietnam, the youngest son of a Confucian scholar-aristocrat who was dismissed from his job as district magistrate for nationalist activity. As a young man, Ho made his way to France and settled in Paris during World War I. He joined the French Socialist party because it was the only party that seriously advocated independence for colonies. In 1919, when Woodrow Wilson and other Allied statesmen were negotiating the treaty of Versailles and the covenant of the League of Nations, Ho spent some of the meager wages that he had earned painting fake Chinese antiques and retouching photos in a Paris studio to rent a set of formal attire and present himself at the Paris Peace Conference. He brought a petition listing the grievances of the Vietnamese against the French colonial regime. But no one would receive him. Ho discovered that Wilson's self-determination applied only to the Czechs and the Poles and other white peoples of Eastern Europe who had been under German or Austro-Hungarian domination. It did not apply to the brown and yellow peoples of Asia or the blacks of Africa.[83]

On August 15, 1945, the same day that Emperor Hirohito announced the surrender of his country over Radio Tokyo, Ho had the Viet Minh representative in Kunming, China, send President Truman a message through the American OSS station there asking the United States, "as a champion of democracy," to make Vietnam an American protectorate "on the same status as the Philippines for an undetermined period" before full independence. He received no reply. Two weeks later, on September 2, 1945, the same day Japanese delegates signed documents of unconditional surrender, Ho read his Vietnamese declaration of independence in Hanoi. Altogether Ho sent Truman and Truman's first secretary of state James Byrnes eleven telegrams and letters of appeal over the eighteen-month period after his establishment of a Vietnamese government in Hanoi. None of these communications were acknowledged. Ho made similar pleas for rescue to Clement Attlee, the prime minister of Britain, to Generalissimo Chiang Kai-shek of Nationalist China and to Joseph Stalin of the Soviet Union. They too did not answer. Thus, Ho and the Viet Minh began their fight against the French in 1945 without any outside help whatsoever. Aid from China only came at the end of 1949 following the victory of Mao Tse-tung over Chiang Kai-shek. Soviet aid to the Viet Minh did not begin until the 1950s. Both China and the Soviet Union only officially recognized the independence of Vietnam in 1950.[84] But even when left completely on their own, Viet Minh forces led by General Vo Nguyen Giap achieved a number of significant victories over the French.[85] This determination of Ho Chi Minh and the Viet Minh to fight the French on their own should have convinced American decision makers that they were no pawns of the Chinese and the Soviets. They should have recognized Ho Chi Minh and General Giap as belonging to a long history of Vietnamese nationalists who believed that they could defeat more powerful invaders of their land because their ancestors had done so many times before. Unfortunately, ignorance of Vietnamese history and culture and the background and character of Ho Chi Minh and the Viet Minh led American decision makers to support the wrong public policy with disastrous results. The mistake was a fundamental one. To arrive at the right public policies, traditional ethics must take into account the relevant local culture or cultures. Hopefully, the failure of U.S. involvement in Vietnam will burn this lesson deeply in people's minds.

In this chapter, I have argued that to meet the challenge of multiculturalism, we must defend an ethics that is secular in character and one that can survive a wide-ranging comparative evaluation of both Western and non-Western moral ideals. I have further argued that there are at least three ways that non-Western cultures can contribute to fashioning an ethics of this sort. First, non-Western moral ideals can help to significantly correct or interpret our Western moral ideals. Second, non-Western cultures can help us recognize important obligations that flow from our moral ideals that we either did not recognize or fully recognize before. Third, non-Western cultures can help us to know how best to apply our own moral ideals, especially cross-culturally. With respect to each of these claims, my argument, of necessity, has been by way of example, drawing on Confucian ethics, American Indian culture and perspectives, and Vietnamese culture to indicate, in specific ways, how traditional ethics can meet the challenge of multiculturalism. Obviously, more work of this sort needs to be done. It is the only way to have a defensible ethics.

5

CONCLUSION

A Peacemaking Way of Doing Philosophy

So what are the implications of the preceding chapters for traditional ethics? In chapter 1, I argued that traditional ethics can establish that moral relativism is an implausible theory, that morality is rationally required and not just rationally permissible, and that there are good reasons for favoring the requirements of a Kantian ethics as I have formulated it. In chapter 2, I argued that the challenge of environmentalism to traditional ethics requires accepting the Principle of Human Defense, the Principle of Human Preservation, the Principle of Disproportionality, and the Principle of Restitution as the appropriate priority or conflict resolution principles to resolve conflicts between humans and nonhuman nature. In chapter 3, I argued that the challenge of feminism requires applying theories of justice, the public/private distinction, and ideals of a morally good person so as to rule out gendered family structures and to implement an ideal of androgyny. In chapter 4, I argued that the challenge of multiculturalism requires a secular ethics that can survive a wide-ranging comparative evaluation of both Western and non-Western moral ideals and cultures.

Yet even if we accept these conclusions, there would still be the question of how, more generally, we should do philosophy, that is, what general attitudes we should bring to philosophy. Let us approach this problem by first seeing how a similar problem arises outside of philosophy or academia generally, specifically how it arises in the media, in politics, and in the practice of law.

The Media, Politics, and the Law

There was a joke going around during Bill Clinton's first term in office. The president went on a fishing trip with members of the press. After their boat left the dock, the president realized he didn't have his tackle so he stepped off the boat and walked to shore, picked up his tackle, and walked back over the surface of the water to the boat. The next day's headline read CLINTON CAN'T SWIM. This joke pokes fun at the tendency of the press to give everything a negative slant, to ignore accomplishments, and to focus on failures. But the tendency is there. Former Republican senator Alan Simpson was taken aback as he chatted with the daughter of old friends, a young woman he had known all her life. She had just graduated from the Columbia University School of Journalism, so Simpson inquired about her plans. "I'm going to be one of the hunters," she announced. "What are you going to hunt?" he asked. "People like you!" was her reply. Thus, today many in the media, at least in the U.S. media, see their role as exposing the weaknesses, failures, slips, and mistakes of public figures. Moreover, editors claim that pieces that are harsh and critical always get the most attention.

But things were not always like this. According to political scientist Larry Sabato, during the Kennedy administration the press was like a lapdog, taking administration press releases at face value. During the Vietnam War and Watergate the press was more like a watchdog, carefully examining the public behavior of public officials, but today the press is most like an attack dog, "constantly chomping at the ankles of public officials every day about everything."[1] But with the media today functioning in this very aggressive manner, focusing on the negative, it has become more and more difficult for the general public to get the whole story and thus be well informed.

The media today, at least the U.S. media, also tend to look for the conflict in any issue or only to cover issues which can be presented as a conflict between two opposing sides. Deborah Lipstadt, who wrote a book about those who deny that the Holocaust took place and the significant news coverage they have received, turned down a number of opportunities to appear on national television, because the invitations were conditional upon her appearing with and debating Holocaust deniers. But not every issue always has two sides that deserve equal billing and many important issues are not best presented as a debate.

If we turn from the media to politics, we find, at least in the United States, a similar emphasis on negativity and conflict rather than on compromise and governance. For example, Speaker Newt Gingrich opposed Clinton's health care plan, reasoning that if the Democrats succeeded in reforming the health care system, they would then be unbeatable. Not surprisingly, a similarly motivated opposition defeated Gingrich's own plan for restructuring Medicare and Medicaid. In the United States, oppositional politics, culminating in Clinton's impeachment trial in the Senate, has reached new levels, and this has not served well the interests of the American people.

Of course, opposition and conflict are at the very heart of the legal adversary system in the United States, as they should be, but even so there is still the question of how far one should go in defense of one's client or to build or prosecute a case against someone. A young lawyer discovered that the firm's client could win a case summarily because the opposing lawyer had missed a statute of limitations date in filing key documents. But the partner in charge of the case refused to use this basis for winning. "We don't practice law like that in this office," he said.[2] But many lawyers would see his action as a failure of proper advocacy.

Proper advocacy, however, has been seen to encompass many things. Philip Morris in its case against ABC over whether the company had deliberately added nicotine to its cigarettes to make sure smokers got hooked, as ABC had reported, delivered twenty-five boxes of requested documents on dark red paper. ABC claimed that the paper was difficult to read and couldn't be scanned into a computer to make its information accessible. They also claimed that the paper gave off an unpleasant odor that made the people who handled it sick.[3] In another lawsuit, one side requested tax returns from the other side, which objected on grounds of privacy. There followed a year and a half of costly litigation going all the way up to the California Supreme Court and back. In the end, the lawyer was compelled to produce the returns, at which time he revealed what he had known all along—his client had no returns for that year.[4] The lawyer had judged that this delaying action was in the interest of his client. In his book *A Civil Action*, Jonathan Harr writes about a well-to-do, real-life lawyer who won a class action suit against W.R. Grace and Beatrice Foods for the dumping of toxic chemicals that polluted the ground water in Woburn, Massachusetts, only after he had lost his home and become destitute.[5] The result in this case is unusual. Usually, the rich side is able to wear down the poor side, but the cause of justice is rarely served by these delaying, obfuscating tactics. On the prosecutorial side, surely the excesses that Kenneth Starr went to in order to build a case against President Clinton, far removed from his initially mandated Whitewater investigation, did not serve well the interests of the American people in having a government focused on solving their important political, economic, and social problems.

The Practice of Philosophy

If we turn now to a more detailed examination of the practice of philosophy, which is our main concern here, we find that doing philosophy is too often modeled on fighting a battle or making war.[6] Arguments are attacked, shot down (like a plane), or sunk (like a ship). Theses are defended, defeated, or demolished (like the walls of a city). Ideas (like people) are killed and destroyed.[7] There are clearly problems with doing philosophy in this way. There is unfairness inherent in the practice, along with its tendency to undercut the possibility of reaching truly justified views, and, as I shall argue, there is a peacemaking alternative. Still the warmaking practice persists.[8]

Just consider what not infrequently takes place at philosophy meetings. A young philosopher is making his first presentation.[9] His paper is in the philosophy of law and his argument relies on a range of judicial decisions. His commentator's objections, which rely on a number of different judicial decisions, are handed to him just before his presentation. Not knowing the particulars of the judicial decisions to which his commentator refers, he is unable to offer a defense of his view. Usually, of course, things are not quite this desperate. Comments do tend to come in late, not infrequently just before the session at which they are to be presented, but speakers do manage some kind of a response, although not a very reflective one. The lateness of the comments, however, does put speakers at a disadvantage with respect to their commentators, and this frequently seems to be an intended result as well. Sometimes commentators do not seem to want to hear the best responses to their critical comments. Rather, what they seem to want to do is win a philosophical battle, triumph in a philosophical war, even at the expense of basic fairness to their philosophical opponents.

Consider some of the other tactics employed by philosophers in pursuit of victory at philosophy meetings. An acquaintance of mine was invited to make a forty-five-minute presentation at a meeting. In working out her thoughts, she discovered that her view could best be defended if her presentation exceeded the time limit by about fifteen minutes, which she decided to do. Her commentator, too, decided that the weaknesses in her view could best be exposed if he exceeded the time limit for commentators. And then my acquaintance chose to respond at length to all of her commentator's criticisms. Thus, in their attempt to triumph one over the other, both deprived their audience of virtually any opportunity to participate in the philosophical debate between them.

Moreover, at philosophy meetings, it is not unheard of for speakers, when they are provided with comments on their papers in advance, to change their papers before presenting them so as to render the comments irrelevant. Some commentators also like to produce a sketch of their comments in advance, get their speakers' reactions if they can, and then revise their comments accordingly. Again, the goal here seems to be victory, even at the expense of basic fairness to their philosophical opponents.

Once, a friend of mine received in advance comments on a paper that she was to present at a colloquium. The comments were apparently devastating and actually quite humorous; they, in effect, invited her to laugh at her own philosophical execution. Her commentator, who happened to be a fairly well-known philosopher, went on to inform her magnanimously that to maximize audience participation he would have nothing further to say at the colloquium after presenting his comments. Yet on the day of the colloquium, when my friend was able to show that her commentator's criticism rested on fairly obvious misreadings of her work and the work of others, her commentator's hand shot up, demanding immediate recognition. Without acknowledging the cogency of her replies, he had a different objection to raise, which he was then able to make the focus of the discussion. What was particularly disappointing for my friend was that after the colloquium had ended, her commentator was no longer interested in discussing their differences any further. This shows how philosophical battles and wars are public affairs. They are enacted for public recognition. There is little behind-the-scenes discussion among the participants to reach agreement. In fact, the participants in philosophical battles and wars may only speak to each other in public confrontations.

I was once asked by a well-known philosopher why I talked to philosophers with whom I radically disagreed. At the time, I was dumbstruck by the question, but now I believe that it reflects the dominant way philosophy is being done these days, and maybe even the dominant way that philosophy has always been done. It sees philosophers as belonging to different groups within which there can be a significant degree of sympathetic understanding but between which there can be only hostile relations, a virtual state of war. If you believe this is the case, then there really is a question about whether you should talk to your philosophical enemies. You may perchance say something that indicates certain problems with your own philosophical view, which may in turn be used against you, and, as a result, you may lose an important philosophical battle and your reputation may decline accordingly.

This warmaking model is not particularly concerned that one face one's strongest opponents. According to this model, the ultimate goal is to win philosophical battles and to triumph in philosophical wars. To achieve this goal, weak opponents will do just as well as strong ones: in fact, weak opponents may even be preferred. Of course, if a strong opponent is on the scene, you must do battle with that opponent. But this warmaking model does not require you to seek out and do battle with your strongest opponents. For this model, what is important is not so much whom you fight, but that you not be defeated.

But what is so bad about doing philosophy this way? Why can't philosophy be seen as "the moral equivalent of war" to use an expression of William James, or "the battleplace of ideas," to alter a phrase associated with John Stuart Mill?[10] I have already indicated the unfairness that accompanies doing philosophy in this way, but an even more significant problem is that this way of doing philosophy undercuts the very possibility of reaching truly justified philosophical views. If those doing philosophy are always trying to win philosophical battles and emerge as victorious, or at least not be defeated, in philosophical wars, they will not be able to achieve the sympathetic understanding of their opponents' views necessary for recognizing what is valuable in those views and what, therefore, needs to be incorporated into their own views. If your goal is always to achieve philosophical victory or to avoid at all costs philosophical defeat, then, given the complexity of philosophical views, it will almost always be possible to rearrange the elements of your views so as to deceive others, and even yourself, about the defensibility of those views, and thereby be able to claim philosophical victory, or at least avoid having to admit to philosophical defeat. For this reason, the warmaking model of doing philosophy renders it difficult to make needed improvements in your philosophical views, or even to abandon them entirely for the sake of better ones. It thereby undercuts the very possibility of your having truly justified philosophical views.

So while philosophers who are committed to the warmaking model of doing philosophy are trying to triumph over their philosophical opponents, their opponents, if they are also committed to the same model, are trying in every way they can, both fair and foul, to avoid having to admit to philosophical defeat. No wonder, then, that so few clear and undeniable philosophical victories emerge from these contests.

But why should warmaking be our model of doing philosophy? Why can't we have a more peaceful and cooperative model? Why

friend should wait for an opportunity to respond to his critique in print in order to set the record straight. Not surprisingly, my friend preferred a different critical strategy. She wanted her critic, when faced with a possible misinterpretation of her text, to reexamine the text to see if it could plausibly be interpreted as she claims to have intended it, and if it could be so interpreted, then the critic should subsequently adopt her preferred interpretation in any critique. In addition to being fairer, this strategy is more likely to focus attention on the most important questions for evaluating a person's work.

Young philosophers in the profession are taught that the quickest way to make a name for themselves is to go after one of the "biggies" in their field and attempt to conclusively refute his or her work, or at least refute part of the work. For some reason, living philosophers are targeted in this way more than dead philosophers, possibly because it then makes it possible to establish a pecking order among existing philosophers. Near the beginning of his career, my dissertation director, Kurt Baier, wrote a book, *The Moral Point of View,* which has become a contemporary classic in ethics. At the time it was published, however, critics jumped upon a single logical mistake that Baier had made in setting out his view. The mistake did not affect the substance of his argument as subsequently was made clear, but that didn't stop a spate of philosophers rushing into print with such titles as "Kurt Baier's 'Logical Lapse'" and "Speculation on the Logical Lapse of Kurt Baier."[12] Certainly, papers with titles like "A Refutation of So and So's Work" are quite likely to find a place at American Philosophical Association meetings. I must confess that, as a younger philosopher, before I knew better, I myself sometimes used this same warmaking strategy to get my own work accepted at APA meetings.

Suppose, then, that we were to adopt a peaceful and cooperative model of doing philosophy which required that we put the most favorable interpretation on the work of others. To do this, we have to listen carefully to those with whom we disagree. Now it might be objected that we are not so much concerned with the views that people actually hold but rather with the best formulations of those views. This is true. We are looking for the most favorable inter-

can't we find points of agreement and attempt to build on the work of others, rather than trying to destroy their work and build anew? Why can't we try to put the most favorable interpretation on the work of others rather than looking for some interpretation with which we can disagree?

One summer, a few years ago I visited a major university to talk to two well-known philosophers about the differences between their views. One of these philosophers had established his reputation as a critic of the other. I talked first to the philosopher whose work had been criticized by his colleague. I asked him, bearing in mind his critic's work, whether he had any objections to interpreting his view in a way that I thought avoided his colleague's criticisms, and he said that he did not. The next day I talked to the philosopher who was known for his critique of his colleague (I was told that they don't talk to each other[11]) and asked him whether he had any objections to the same interpretation of his colleague's work, mentioning that his colleague had just accepted this interpretation the day before. He said that he did not. Yet it turns out that this same philosopher was hard at work on a book in which he was criticizing yet another interpretation of his colleague's work—a book in which the more favorable interpretation of his colleague's work was never mentioned.

Commentators at philosophy meetings almost invariably start out by saying that there are many things with which they agree in the work they are commenting on, but *in their role as commentators,* they will focus on that with which they disagree. This compelling need to find something with which to disagree can lead to over-simplifying a person's work, distorting it, or unsympathetically interpreting it. And there are alternative interpretative strategies available to commentators. They can draw out the implications of a person's work, compare it to the work of others, find additional arguments for the person's conclusions, or repair defects in it. Thus, commentators are not forced to adopt a strategy of slash and burn.

A friend of mine responding to a critic at a philosophy conference claimed that her work had been misinterpreted. Her critic in subsequent work refused to give up his "misinterpretation," claiming that others might make the same misinterpretation and so my

pretations of particular views. Nevertheless, in order to get at the most favorable interpretations, it is usually necessary to listen carefully to those who actually hold particular views, because they are in a good position to determine what are the most favorable interpretations of those views.

We also need to reach out and try to understand those who have views of which we are ignorant. But this can be harder to do than one thinks. For example, another friend of mine recently presented a paper to the philosophy department at a major midwestern university. It was in fact the first paper to deal with feminism to be presented to that department. Her commentator, a recent Ph.D. from an Ivy League university, produced a set of comments, almost as long as her paper, that focused entirely on the welfare-liberal section of her paper. After the session, her commentator was asked by a female graduate student why he had not commented at all on the feminist part of her paper. He replied that he knew very little about feminism, and so he thought it best for him to focus on what he did know much more about. Apparently, the rest of the faculty attending the session felt the same way, since although they raised numerous questions, their questions too focused entirely on the welfare-liberal section of her paper. What this shows is that it is very difficult to get philosophers to inform themselves about challenging new areas like feminism. The department to which my friend presented her paper was particularly deficient in this regard because, while its members remained generally ignorant of feminist philosophy, they also refused to appoint anyone to their fairly large department whose primary area of expertise was feminist philosophy.

Moreover, until we make philosophy a more peaceful and cooperative venture, the numbers of women in the profession, at least in the United States, may not go much beyond the 25 percent it has been hovering at for years.[13] There is considerable evidence that girls and women are more attracted to a peacemaking and cooperative way of doing academic work than they are to the warmaking alternative.[14] So in addition to being fairer and more likely to attain justified belief or truth, the possibility of also making the profession more friendly to women provides just one more reason for moving toward a more peacemaking, cooperative way of doing philosophy.

The Requirements of a Peacemaking Way of Doing Philosophy

We can now characterize more fully a peacemaking way of doing philosophy. It is a way of doing philosophy that while seeking to determine what are the most justified views is committed to

1. a fair-mindedness that, among other things, puts the most favorable interpretation on the views of one's opponents,
2. an openness that reaches out to understand challenging new views,
3. a self-criticalness that requires modifying or abandoning one's views should the weight of available evidence require it.

Now it might be objected that if the most favorable interpretation is placed upon a warmaking way of doing philosophy, it too can be seen to incorporate roughly the same desirable features as a peacemaking alternative. Thus, in pursuing victory, a warmaking way of doing philosophy could be seen to require

1. a fair-mindedness that among other things, puts the most favorable interpretation on the views of one's opponents so that one's victories are won fair and square,
2. an openness that reaches out to understand challenging new views so that victories are not obtained for lack of worthy opponents,
3. a self-criticalness that requires admitting defeat should the weight of available evidence require it.

Obviously, a warmaking way of doing philosophy that is characterized in this way is practically indistinguishable from its peacemaking alternative. What this shows is that there will be good reasons to favor a peacemaking way of doing philosophy over a warmaking alternative only when the latter is understood and practiced, as it unfortunately usually is understood and practiced, to be the pursuit of winning or avoiding defeat above all else, with all the unfairness and deceitfulness that such a pursuit involves.

There is also the question of what philosophers committed to a peacemaking way of doing philosophy as I have characterized it are supposed to do when confronted with philosophers who seem to be committed to this objectionable form of a warmaking way of doing philosophy. Obviously, this question is similar to the question of what peaceful nations or individuals are supposed to do when confronted with seemingly belligerent nations or individuals, and, not surprisingly, the answer in each case seems to be similar as well. Surely, peacemaking philosophers should not give up their commitment to the fair-mindedness, openness, and self-criticalness that make their way of doing philosophy defensible. At the same time, they can justifiably protect themselves against the unfairness and deceitfulness of those committed to this objectionable form of a warmaking philosophy, as well as strive in every way they can to expose the inadequacies of this way of doing philosophy as a method for attaining the most defensible philosophical views. Needless to say, in many ways, the future success of philosophy will depend on just how successful peacemaking philosophers turn out to be in these endeavors.

When I first introduced the contrast between warmaking and peacemaking ways of doing philosophy in the course of presenting my own work, I was surprised at the responses of my audiences. This is because on such occasions the questions and comments were uniformly friendly and constructive. I thought that somehow I must have failed to communicate well because so few in my audiences seemed bent on simply attacking my central arguments. Even fairly critical points directed at those same arguments were frequently accompanied by suggestions as to how the criticisms might be met. Could it be, then, that by drawing attention to these two contrasting ways of doing philosophy, one could actually lead one's audience to react to one's work in a peacemaking rather than a warmaking manner? It is an intriguing possibility.

Consider how this might apply to yourself. Suppose you were to ask yourself the following questions:

1. Have you given this book the kind of attention necessary to assess its arguments and conclusions fairly?
2. Were you open to being informed by the discussion of topics in the book with which you are unfamiliar or positions with which you disagree?
3. When you found that you had objections to some of the arguments or conclusions of the work, did you try to uncover effective ways to respond to your own objections?
4. Finally, but most important, did you approach the book entertaining the possibility that you might modify or abandon your previous views should the arguments of the book appear compelling?

Obviously, only if you can answer yes to all of these questions would you, in fact, be truly committed to a peacemaking way of doing philosophy.

No doubt it is a bit unusual for an author to put readers on the spot like this by raising such challenging questions for them. But if the objectionable warmaking model of doing philosophy is to lose the hold it has on contemporary philosophical discussion, unusual steps will have to be taken. From this perspective, then, it seems far from inappropriate to inform one's readers what is required to apply this peacemaking way of doing philosophy to the reading of one's own book. In fact, given an author's commitment to this peacemaking way of doing philosophy, it is just what he or she should be doing.

NOTES

Chapter 1: Introduction

1. I am using "environmentalism" here in a somewhat idiosyncratic way. One might think that the term denotes the view that the natural environment should be protected and its destruction and pollution prevented, but, as I am using the term, this view also affirms that at least some nonhuman living beings should count in their own right and not just as a means to human welfare. Unfortunately, there is no term currently in use that has such a general denotation. Animal liberation, the land ethic, biocentrism, and deep ecology are all versions of environmentalism as I am using the term. In addition, failure to count nonhuman living beings in this noninstrumental fashion is to be biased in favor of humans, and environmentalism, as I am using the term, maintains that this bias is omnipresent in traditional ethics.

2. See Knud Rasmussen, *The People of the Polar North* (London: Kegan Paul, 1908), pp. 106ff.; and Peter Freuchen, *Book of the Eskimos* (New York: World Publishing Company, 1961, pp. 193–206. And cf. Hans Reusch, *Top of the World* (New York: Pocket Books, 1951), pp. 123–26.

3. See Mary Douglas, *Purity and Danger* (London: Praeger, 1966), p. 39.

4. It may be possible, however, to show that even those who deny that the fetus is a person should still oppose abortion in a wide range of cases. See my "Abortion and the Rights of Distant Peoples and Future Generations," *The Journal of Philosophy* 77 (1980), pp. 424–40; *How to Make People Just* (Totowa: Rowman and Littlefield, 1988), and "Response to Nine Commentators," *The Journal of Social Philosophy* 22 (1991), pp. 100–118.

5. This is not to deny that it would have been a good thing to avoid carcinogens in the Middle Ages; it is just that without the concept of a carcinogen, there couldn't have been any moral requirement to do so.

6. For more on this requirement, see my *Contemporary Social and Political Philosophy* (Belmont: Wadsworth, 1995), pp. 2–5. It should also be pointed out that this requirement necessitates interpreting the Kantian notion of acts

that accord with duty in particular circumstances as acts that certain moral agents, but not necessarily all moral agents, would have a duty to do in those circumstances.

7. See W. T. Stace, *The Concept of Morals* (New York: Macmillan, 1937), chapters 1 and 2.

8. These problems that the moral relativist faces in specifying what morality is relative to are analogous to problems that the opponent of moral relativism faces in specifying whose interests morality should take into account. For example, should morality take into account just the interests of all humans, or more expansively, the interests of all sentient beings, or more expansively still, the interests all living beings? In chapter 2, we will be discussing how the opponent of moral relativism should deal with these analogous problems.

9. For further argument on this point, see Marcus Singer, *Generalization in Ethics* (New York: Knopf, 1961), chapter 2, and Alan Gewirth, "The Non-Trivializability of Universalizability," *Australasian Journal of Philosophy* (1969), pp. 123–31.

10. Jesse Kalin, "In Defense of Egoism," in *Morality and Rational Self-Interest,* ed. David Gauthier (Englewood Cliffs: Prentice-Hall, 1970), pp. 73–74.

11. For additional reasons why ethical egoism is a consistent view, see my article "Ethical Egoism and Beyond," *Canadian Journal of Philosophy* (1979), pp. 91–108.

12. From here on, I will use "egoist" and "egoism" as short for "universal ethical egoist" and "universal ethical egoism".

13. "Ought" presupposes "can" here. So unless people have the capacity to entertain and follow both self-interested and moral reasons for acting, it does not make any sense asking whether they ought or ought not to do so. Moreover, moral reasons here are understood to necessarily include (some) altruistic reasons but not necessarily to exclude (all) self-interested reasons. So the question of whether it would be rational for us to follow self-interested reasons rather than moral reasons should be understood as the question of whether it would be rational for us to follow self-interested reasons exclusively rather than some appropriate set of self-interested reasons and altruistic reasons which constitutes the class of moral reasons.

14. I understand the pure altruist to be the mirror image of the pure egoist. Whereas the pure egoist thinks that the interests of others count for them but not for herself except instrumentally, the pure altruist thinks that her own interests count for others but not for herself except instrumentally.

15. For a discussion of the causal links involved here, see *Marketing and Promotion of Infant Formula in Developing Countries*. Hearing before the Subcommittee of International Economic Policy and Trade of the Committee on Foreign Affairs, U.S. House of Representatives, 1980. See also Maggie McComas et al., *The Dilemma of Third World Nutrition* (1983).

16. Assume that both jobs have the same beneficial effects on the interests of others.

17. I am assuming that acting contrary to reason is a significant failing with respect to the requirements of reason, and that there are many ways of not acting in (perfect) accord with reason that do not constitute acting contrary to reason.

18. Otherwise, they would really fall under the classification of aesthetic reasons.

19. Of course, such reasons would have to be taken into account at some point in a complete justification for morality, but the method of integrating such reasons into a complete justification of morality would simply parallel the method already used for integrating self-interested and altruistic reasons. In Chapter 2, I will consider how reasons that promote nonhuman welfare should be integrated into a defensible ethics.

20. This is because, as I shall argue, morality itself already represents a compromise between egoism and altruism. So to ask that moral reasons be weighed against self-interested reasons is, in effect, to count self-interested reasons twice—once in the compromise between egoism and altruism and again when moral reasons are weighed against self-interested reasons. But to count self-interested reasons twice is clearly objectionable.

21. Assume that all these methods of waste disposal have roughly the same amount of beneficial effects on the interests of others.

22. Notice that by "egoistic perspective" here I mean the view that grants the prima facie relevance of both egoistic and altruistic reasons to rational choice and then tries to argue for the superiority of egoistic reasons. Similarly by "altruistic perspective" I mean the view that grants the prima facie relevance of both egoistic and altruistic reasons to rational choice and then tries to argue for the superiority of altruistic reasons.

23. For further discussion, see my *Justice for Here and Now* (New York: Cambridge University Press, 1998), chapter 2.

24. See R. Duncan Luce and Howard Raiffa, *Games and Decisions* (New York: John Wiley, 1967), chapter 13.

25. I am assuming that neither of these sides has non-question-begging grounds for its assumption.

26. Actually, all of what pure altruism holds is:
   (1) All high-ranking altruistic reasons have priority over conflicting lower-ranking self-interested reasons.
   (2) All low-ranking altruistic reasons have priority over conflicting higher-ranking self-interested reasons.
   (3) All high-ranking altruistic reasons have priority over conflicting high-ranking self-interested reasons.
   (4) All low-ranking altruistic reasons have priority over conflicting low-ranking self-interested reasons.

By contrast, all of what egoism holds is:
   (1') All high-ranking self-interested reasons have priority over conflicting lower-ranking altruistic reasons.
   (2') All low-ranking self-interested reasons have priority over conflicting higher-ranking altruistic reasons.
   (3') All high-ranking self-interested reasons have priority over conflicting high-ranking altruistic reasons.
   (4') All low-ranking self-interested reasons have priority over conflicting high-ranking altruistic reasons.

And what the compromise view holds is (1) and (1') and it favors neither pure altruism nor egoism with respect to (3) and (4), (3') and (4').

27. Notice that even if one were to take this perspective, it would still follow that the egoistic and altruistic perspectives beg the question against the other to a far greater extent than the compromise view does against either of them because the whole of what egoism holds about the priority of reasons, that is, (1) and (2), is in conflict with an altruistic perspective and the whole of what altruism holds about the priority of reasons, that is, (1') and (2'), is in conflict with an egoistic perspective. Consequently, even viewed this way, the compromise view, on grounds of being least question-begging would still be the rationally preferable resolution. (As you may have suspected or maybe known from my previous work, this was the way I used to justify the compromise view, before I recognized that it could be given a completely non-question-begging justification.)

28. Thomas Scanlon discusses this problem in *What We Owe to Others* (Cambridge, Harvard University Press, 1998), chapter 3.

29. For further argument, see my book *Justice for Here and Now* (New York: Cambridge University Press, 1998), chapter 2.

30. Obviously, other moral approaches to practical problems could be distinguished, but I think the three I will be considering reflect the range of possible approaches that are relevant to the resolution of these problems.

31. In fact, the debate as to whether African Americans are better off now because of the programs of the Great Society has taken a more scholarly turn. See Charles Murray, *Losing Ground* (New York: Basic Books, 1984), and Christopher Jencks, "How Poor Are the Poor?" *New York Review of Books,* May 9, 1985.

32. This form also has clear roots in Aristotle. See his *Nicomachean Ethics,* Book II, 1107a, 10–25.

33. For further discussion, see my book *How to Make People Just* (Totowa: Rowman and Littlefield, 1988), chapter 4.

Chapter 2: Environmentalism

1. Peter Singer, *Animal Liberation,* rev. ed. (New York, Avon Books, 1992).

2. Bernard Rollins, *Animal Rights and Human Morality,* 2nd ed. (New York: Prometheus Books, 1992), chapter 3.; Alex Fino, *Lethal Laws* (New York: Zed Books, 1997), chapter 1.

3. Tom Regan, *The Case for Animal Rights* (Berkeley: University of California Press, 1983).

4. Paul Taylor, *Respect for Nature* (Princeton: Princeton University Press, 1986), pp. 68–71 and p. 17.

5. Ibid., pp. 68–71.

6. One way to think about species is as ongoing genetic lineages sequentially embodied in different organisms. See Lawrence Johnson, *A Morally Deep World* (New York: Cambridge University Press, 1991), p.156, Holmes Rolston III, *Environmental Ethics,* chapter 4.

7. Ecosystems can be simple or complex, stable or unstable, and they can suffer total collapse. Following Lawrence Johnson, we can go on to characterize moral subjects as living systems in a persistent state of low entropy sustained by metabolic processes for accumulating energy whose organic unity and self-identity is maintained in equilibrium by homeostatic feedback processes. See his *A Morally Deep World,* chapter 6. Happily, this definition distinguishes moral subjects (living systems) from cars, refrigerators,

etc. On this point, see my article "A Biocentrist Fights Back," *Environmental Ethics* (Winter 1998), 361–76, where I also entertain some doubts about whether ecosystems have a good of their own and discuss why this would not lead to different practical implications for biocentric pluralism.

8. *Respect for Nature,* pp. 71–80.

9. Ibid., pp. 99–168.

10. Ibid., pp. 129–56.

11. Assuming God exists, humans might also be better off if they could retain their distinctive traits while acquiring one or another of God's qualities, but consideration of this possibility and other related possibilities would take us too far afield. Nonhumans might also be better off it they could retain their distinctive traits and acquire one or another of the distinctive traits possessed by the members of other nonhuman species.

12. This assumes that there is an environmental niche that cheetahs can fill.

13. Notice also that, on Taylor's account, even when the members of a particular species would be better off having some additional trait, it would not follow that they thereby have greater intrinsic moral worth.

14. *Respect for Nature,* pp. 134–35.

15. Ibid., pp. 154–168.

16. This formulation also extends the argument to all living beings, including species and ecosystems.

17. The previous argument has established that we do not have any non-question-begging reasons to treat humans as superior overall to other living beings, by showing that the reasons that are standardly given for human superiority do not meet the standard of non-question-beggingness. What I have not established, of course, is that it would be impossible for us to have any such reasons because no such reasons can be given, but it seems to me that the burden of proof here is not on me to demonstrate the impossibility of there being any reasons of this sort, but rather the burden of proof is on those who would use an appeal to human superiority to justify aggressing against nonhuman nature.

18. Strictly speaking, not to treat humans as superior overall to other living beings is to treat them as either equal overall, *or inferior overall,* to other living beings, but I am using equal overall to include both of these possibilities since neither possibility involves the domination of nonhuman nature; moreover, the latter possibility is an unlikely course of action for humans to take. It also follows from (2) that not to treat humans as superior

overall to other living beings is not to aggress against them by sacrificing their basic needs to meet the nonbasic needs of humans.

19. Ibid., pp. 47–53, 154.

20. Ibid., chapter 6.

21. Ibid., pp. 264–69.

22. For the purposes of this chapter, I will follow the convention of excluding humans from the denotation of "animals."

23. For an account of what constitutes justifiably held property within human ethics, see my *How to Make People Just* (Totowa: Roman and Littlefield, 1988).

24. Of course, one might contend that no principle of human defense applies in traditional ethics because either "nonviolent pacifism" or "nonlethal pacifism" is the most morally defensible view. However, I have argued elsewhere that this is not the case, and that still other forms of pacifism more compatible with just war theory are also more morally defensible than either of these forms of pacifism. See my book *Justice for Here and Now* (New York: Cambridge University Press, 1998), chapter 7.

25. Notice too that the Principle of Human Defense permits defending oneself and other human beings against the harmful aggression of individual animals and plants or whole species or ecosystems, even when this only serves the nonbasic needs of humans.

26. The Principle of Human Preservation also imposes a limit on when we can defend nonhuman living beings from human aggression.

27. For further discussion of basic needs, see my *How to Make People Just*, pp. 45ff.

28. It should be pointed out that the Principle of Human Preservation must be implemented in a way that causes the least harm possible, which means that, other things being equal, basic needs should be met by aggressing against nonsentient rather than against sentient living beings so as to avoid the pain and suffering that would otherwise be inflicted on sentient beings.

29. It is important to recognize here that we also have a strong obligation to prevent lifeboat cases from arising in the first place.

30. It should also be pointed out that the Principle of Human Preservation does not support an unlimited right of procreation. In fact, the theory of justice presupposed here gives priority to the basic needs of existing beings over the basic needs of future possible beings, and this should effectively limit (human) procreation.

31. *Respect for Nature*, pp. 269–91.

32. Ibid., p. 274.

33. Ibid., p. 276.

34. It is important to recognize that relying on an account of basic needs here does not presuppose any essentialist theory of human nature. See my *How to Make People Just*, p. 45ff.

35. This principle is clearly acceptable to welfare liberals and socialists, and it can even be shown to be acceptable to libertarians by an argument I have developed at length elsewhere. See *Justice for Here and Now*, chapter 3.

36. Of course, libertarians have claimed that we can recognize that people have equal basic rights while failing to meet, but not sacrificing, the basic needs of other human beings. However, I have argued at length that this claim is mistaken. See the reference in the previous note.

37. It should be pointed out that although the Principle of Disproportionality prohibits aggressing against the basic needs of individual animals or plants, or of whole species or ecosystems, the Principle of Human Defense permits defending oneself and other human beings against the harmful aggression of animals and plants or even whole species or ecosystems, even when this only serves the nonbasic needs of humans. The underlying idea is that we can legitimately promote our nonbasic needs by *defending* our persons and our property against the aggression of nonhuman others but not by *aggressing* against them. In the case of human aggression, a slightly weaker principle of defense holds: We can legitimately promote our nonbasic needs by defending our persons and property except when the aggression is undertaken as the only way to meet basic human needs.

38. It might be objected here that this argument is speciesist in that it permits humans to aggress against nonhuman nature whenever it is necessary for meeting our own basic needs or the basic needs of humans we happen to care about. But this objection surely loses some of its force once it is recognized that it is also permissible for us to aggress against the nonbasic needs of humans whenever it is necessary for meeting our own basic needs or the basic needs of humans we happen to care about.

39. Aldo Leopold's view is usually interpreted as holistic in this sense. Leopold wrote "A thing is right when it tends to preserve the integrity, stability and beauty of the biotic community. It is wrong when it tends otherwise." See his *A Sand County Almanac* (Oxford: Oxford University Press, 1949).

40. Paul Taylor has always been considered a defender of the individualist view.

41. I am assuming that in these cases of conflict, the good of *other* human beings is not at issue. Otherwise, as we have already noted, other considerations will apply. It may also be the case that whenever there is considerable harm to other species, ecosystems, or to some degree the whole biotic community, there will be considerable harm to humans as well and so such actions could be prohibited on such grounds.

42. For example, it is now quite clear that our war with Iraq could have been avoided if early on we had refused to support the military buildup of Saddam Hussein.

43. Moreover, depending on how one assesses the impact of humans upon the whole biotic community, requiring humans to be saints and sacrifice their basic needs whenever they conflict with the greater good of the whole biotic community could be quite demanding, for example, it could demand that humans decimate their numbers for the greater good of the whole biotic community. There are reasonable demands that fall far short of this, however: for one thing, for the good of the whole biotic community humans *are* required to put into effect a strong population control policy.

44. Where it is most likely to be morally required is where our negligent actions have caused the environmental problem in the first place.

45. Of course, one remains free to sacrifice one's basic needs here if that is what one wants to do.

46. Actually, in traditional ethics, taking away the means of survival from people who justly possess them is not morally justified even when it is needed for one's own survival. Again, this is grounded in the altruistic forbearance that we can reasonably expect of humans. This is a different case from the lifeboat case, discussed earlier, in which the human individuals are all trying to acquire the yet unowned means of survival when there is not enough for all.

47. Singer's *Animal Liberation* (New York: Avon Books, 1975) inspired this view. According to holists, the good of a species or the good of an ecosystem or the good of the whole biotic community can trump the good of individual living beings.

48. Baird Callicott, "Animal Liberation: A Triangular Affair," *Environmental Ethics* 2 (1980), 311–28.

49. Mark Sagoff, "Animal Liberation and Environmental Ethics: Bad Marriage, Quick Divorce," *Osgood Hall Law Journal* 22 (1984), 297–307.

50. Mary Ann Warren, "The Rights of the Nonhuman World," in *Environmental Philosophy,* ed. by Robert Elliot and Arran Gare (University Park:

Penn State University Press, 1983), 109–34; Baird Callicott, *In Defense of the Land Ethic* (Albany: State University Press of New York, 1989) chapter 3. See also Warren's *Moral Status* (New York: Oxford University Press, 1997).

51. U.S. Department of Agriculture, Economic Research Service, as quoted in Frances Moore Lappe, *Diet for a Small Planet* (New York: Ballantine Books, 1982) p. 69.

52. Robin Hur as quoted in Lappe, p. 80.

53. For the grounds for meeting our basic nutritional needs in ways that prevent animal pain and suffering, see note 28.

54. Sagoff, "Animal Liberation and Environmental Ethics," pp. 301–5.

55. There is an analogous story to tell here about "domesticated" plants, but there is no analogous story to tell about "extra humans" who could be raised for food, given that the knowledge these "extra humans" would have of their fate would most likely make their lives not worth living. But even assuming that this is not the case, with the consequence that this particular justification for domestication is ruled out because of its implications for a similar use of humans, it still would be the case that domestication is justified in a sustainable agriculture to provide fertilizer for crops to meet basic human needs.

56. Of course, if we permitted farmland and grazing land to return to its natural state, certain wild animals would surely benefit as a result, but why should we be required to favor the interests of these wild animals over the interests of farm animals, especially when favoring the latter serves our own interests as well? It should also be pointed out that the animals that would benefit under these different policies are primarily animals that would come into existence if the policies were carried out. For further discussion, see Bart Gruzalski, "The Case against Raising and Killing Animals for Food," in H. Miller and W. Williams, *Ethics and Animals* (Clifton, N.J.: Humana Press, 1983), pp. 251–63.

57. See Ann Causey, "On the Morality of Hunting," *Environmental Ethics* (1989), pp. 327–43.

58. For further critique and defense of Regan's and Singer's views, see Dale Jamieson, "Rights, Justice and Duties to Provide Assistance: A Critique of Regan's Theory of Rights," *Ethics* (1990), pp. 349–62; S. F. Sapontzis, *Morals, Reason and Animals* (Philadelphia: Temple University Press, 1987), especially chapter 13.

59. For an argument for rejecting the second horn of this dilemma, see my paper "Reconciling Anthropocentric and Nonanthropocentric Environmental Ethics," *Environmental Values* (1994), pp. 229–44.

60. Another way to put the central claim here is say that species equality rules out domination, where domination here means aggressing against the basic needs of other living beings for the sake of satisfying nonbasic needs. So understood, species equality does not rule out treating species differently, even preferring one's basic needs, or the basic needs of one's species to the basic needs of nonhuman individuals, species, and whole ecosystems.

61. I am not objecting here to all attempts to derive, or better ground, "values" on "facts" but just to the arbitrariness that seems to characterize the one under consideration. For a discussion of what good derivations or groundings of values would look like, see Kurt Baier, *The Rational and the Moral Order* (Chicago: Open Court, 1995), chapter 1.

62. Although the living beings must be capable of being benefited and harmed, unlike cars, refrigerators, etc., in a nonderivative way. See my article,"A Biocentrist Fights Back."

63. One notable exception to the requirement of independence are some species and subspecies of domesticated animals who have been made into beings who are dependent for their survival on humans. I contend that because of their historic interaction with these domesticated animals, humans have acquired a positive obligation to care for these animals provided certain mutually beneficial arrangements can be maintained.

64. Even the requirement that those who can be benefited or harmed in a nonderivative way must have a certain independence to their lives or a good of their own is, on my account, *derived* from what we can reasonably expect of moral agents.

65. For further discussion of this fundamental characterization of morality (1), see *Justice for Here and Now,* chapter 3.

66. This argument actually subsumes the argument given earlier in this chapter for species equality given that its key premises can also be derived from (1).

67. This view is discussed in Lynn White's "The Historical Roots of our Ecological Crisis," *Science* (1967), pp. 1203–7.

68. See Lloyd Steffen, "In Defense of Dominion," *Environmental Ethics* (1992), pp. 63–80; Eileen Flynn, *Cradled in Human Hands* (Kansas City, 1991), chapter 3; Robin Attfield, *The Ethics of Environmental Concern* (New York: Columbia University Press, 1983), chapter 2.

69. But even here there is not a coincidence of interest for all species. Certain types of bacteria, for example, thrive in oxygen-depleted environments.

70. It is also the case that biocentric pluralism provides a morally superior argument against the domination of nonhuman nature to what is provided by a completely human-centered environmental ethics. To see this, suppose someone were to argue that slavery was a bad system because you couldn't make as much money using slaves as you could employing free workers because the latter would do a better job for you. Surely, even if this were the case, we would not think that it was the best argument against slavery. Surely, the best argument against slavery is that it denies human beings their most fundamental rights. Similarly, even if the domination of nonhuman nature is bad for humans, as it is to some extent, the best argument against that domination is that it fails to respect the moral status of nonhuman nature.

Chapter 3: Feminism

1. Carol Gilligan, *In a Different Voice* (Cambridge: Harvard University Press, 1982).

2. It is commonly agreed upon among feminists that traditional ethics is biased against women and that this bias is manifested in the ways I suggest, but some feminists have argued that this bias is manifested in still other ways. For example, see Virginia Held, "Feminist Transformations of Moral Theory," in James P. Sterba, *Ethics: The Big Questions* (Oxford: Blackwell, 1998), pp. 331–45; Alison Jaggar, "Western Feminist Ethics," in *The Blackwell Guide to Ethics,* ed. Hugh LaFollette (Oxford: Blackwell, 2000), pp. 348–74. Nevertheless, I think that all would agree that if the correctives I propose in this chapter were implemented then virtually all forms of bias against women in traditional ethics would be corrected as well.

3. Carol Gilligan, "Moral Orientations and Moral Development," in *Women and Moral Theory,* ed. Eva Kittay and Diana Meyers (Totowa: Rowman and Littlefield, 1987), p. 23

4. Ibid., p. 25.

5. Jean Grimshaw, *Philosophy and Feminist Thinking* (Minneapolis: University of Minnesota Press, 1986); James P. Sterba, *How to Make People Just* (Totowa: Rowman and Littlefield, 1988), pp. 182–4; Will Kymlicka, *Contemporary Political Philosophy* (New York: Oxford, 1990), chapter 7; Claudia Card, ed., *Feminist Ethics* (Lawrence: University of Kansas Press, 1991); Eve Browning Cole and Susan Coultrap-McQuin, eds., *Exploration in Feminist Ethics* (Bloomington: Indiana University Press, 1992); Virginia Held, ed.,

Justice and Care (Boulder: Westview, 1995); Daryl Koehn, *Rethinking Feminist Ethics* (New York: Routledge, 1998).

6. Ibid., p. 20.

7. Ibid., p. 23; *In a Different Voice,* pp. 100, 149.

8. Kittay and Meyers, p. 5.

9. Virginia Held, "Caring Relations and Principles of Justice," in *Controversies in Feminism,* ed. by James P. Sterba (Lanham: Rowman and Littlefield, 2000).

10. Claudia Card, "Particular Justice and General Care," in *Controversies in Feminism,* ed. by James P. Sterba (Lanham: Rowman and Littlefield, 2000).

11. Or maybe we should regard this as a case where one requirement of (particular) justice that the father give his child what he or she deserves has priority over another requirement of (particular) justice that he provide more of his students the help they need.

12. We can also view such conflicts as conflicts between (universal) care and a (particular) care.

13. Of course, we need an account of when a particularist perspective has priority over a universalist perspective and vice versa, but that is a separate issue. My own view is that the issue of priority has to be resolved in a way that is justified to all affacted parties. See my *How to Make People Just,* pp. 80–82.

14. John Rawls, *A Theory of Justice,* (Cambridge: Harvard University Press, 1971), pp. 19, 491.

15. Ibid., p. 490.

16. John Rawls, *Political Liberalism* (New York: Columbia University Press, 1993). Some of the papers that Rawls published after *A Theory of Justice* that are not directly incorporated into *Political Liberalism* are the following: "Reply to Lyons and Teitelman," *Journal of Philosophy* (1972);"Some Reasons for the Maximin Criterion," *American Economic Review* (1974); "Reply to Alexander and Musgrave, " *Quarterly Journal of Economics* (1974); "The Independence of Moral Theory," in *Proceedings of the American Philosophical Association* (1974–5); "A Kantian Conception of Equality," *Cambridge Review* (1975); "Fairness to Goodness," *Philosophical Review* (1975); "Social Unity and Primary Goods," in *Utilitarianism and Beyond,* Amartya Sen and Bernard Williams, eds. (Cambridge: Cambridge University Press, 1982).

17. Susan Okin, *Justice, Gender and the Family* (New York: Basic Books, 1989), chapter 5.

18. See Stephanie Coontz, *The Way We Never Were* (New York: Basic Books, 1992), pp. 2–3, 16; Michael Wolff, *Where We Stand* (New York: Bantam Books, 1992), pp. 23ff., 115; Deirdre English, "Through the Glass Ceiling," *Mother Jones,* November 1992; *USA Today,* October 1–3, 1999. For the first time in twenty years, the percentage of poor children has dropped below 20 percent.

19. See, for example, the essays in *Feminism and Families,* ed. Hilde Lindemann Nelson (New York: Routledge, 1997).

20. John Rawls, "The Idea of Public Reason Revisited," *University of Chicago Law Review* (1997), pp. 787–94. Interestingly, Martha Nussbaum cites Rawls along with Susan Okin as a contemporary theorist of the family who has "asked how legal changes could promote respect for women's worth and autonomy, and ensure norms of fair equality of opportunity," but the only reference to Rawls other than to his *A Theory of Justice,* which merely assumes that families are just, is to an unpublished manuscript. See her *Cultivating Humanity* (Cambridge: Harvard University Press, 1997), p.196 and note 11.

21. Ibid., pp. 789–90.

22. Ibid., p. 792.

23. Paula England, ed., *Theory on Gender/Feminism on Theory* (New York: Aldine De Gruyter, 1993).

24. *New York Times,* October 25, 1999; Sheila Kamerman, "Starting Right: What We Owe Our Children Under Three," *The American Prospect,* Winter 1991; Ruth Sidel, "Day Care: Do We Really Care?" in *Issues in Feminism,* ed. by Sheila Ruth (Mountain View, Calif.: Mayfield, 1990), p. 342. At present 99 percent of private U.S. employers still do not offer day care to their employees. See Susan Faludi, *Backlash* (New York: Crown Publishing Co., 1988) p.xiii; *New York Times,* November 25, 1987.

25. Amitai Etzioni, *The Spirit of Community* (Crown Publishers, 1993), chapter 2.

26. *Mother Jones,* May/June 1991: *New York Times*, November 25, 1987; Ruth Sidel, "Day Care: Do We Really Care?" See also Phyllis Moen, *Woman's Two Roles* (New York: Auburn House, 1992). According to one nationwide study by an agency of the U.S. Department of Labor, 1 percent of day care facilities were "superior," 15 percent were "good," 35 percent were essentially "custodial" or "fair," and nearly half were considered "poor." See Sidel, p. 341. See also Cost, Quality and Child Outcomes Study Team, *Cost, Quality and Child Outcomes in Child Care Centers,* 2nd ed. (Denver: University of Colorado Pres, 1995).

27. See Lenore Weitzman, *The Divorce Revolution: The Unexpected Social and Economic Consequences for Women and Children in America* (New York: Free Press, 1985).

28. Dorothy Dinnerstein, *The Mermaid and the Minotaur* (New York: Harper and Row, 1977); Nancy Chodorow, *Mothering: Psychoanalysis and the Sociology of Gender* (Berkeley: University of California Press, 1978); Vivian Gornick, "Here's News: Fathers Matter as Much as Mothers," *Village Voice,* October 13, 1975.

29. Amitai Etzioni, *The Spirit of Community,* chapter 2.

30. *In These Times,* February 22, 1993.

31. Ibid.

32. *New York Times,* February 16, 1998.

33. Women's Action Coalition, *WAC Stats: The Facts About Women* (New York: New Press, 1993), p. 60. According to another study, wives employed in the labor force do approximately twenty-nine hours of domestic labor a week, in addition to their labor market jobs, Wives not in the labor force do between thirty-two and fifty-six hours of domestic labor a week, with the differences largely due to the presence of young children. Overall, husbands spend approximately eleven hours a week in domestic labor, regardless of whether or not their wives are in the labor force. See Shelley Coverman, "Women's Work Is Never Done," in *Women: A Feminist Perspective,* 4th ed., ed. Jo Freeman (Mountain View, Calif.: Mayfield, 1989) pp. 356–68. Research on whether men are increasing their contribution has not yet substantiated a significant increase, but one study did find an increase of eleven minutes a day for husband's domestic labor. See also Joni Hersch and Leslie Stratton, "Housework, Wages, and the Division of Housework Time for Employed Spouses," *AEA Papers and Proceedings* 84 (1994), pp. 120–25.

34. Sharon Lloyd, "Situating a Feminist Criticism of John Rawls's *Political Liberalism,*" *Loyola of Los Angeles Law Review* 28 (1995), pp.1338–43.

35. Richard Arneson, "Feminism and Family Justice," *Public Affairs Quarterly* 11:4, October 1997, pp. 318–9.

36. This is assuming that there are many diverse positions and roles needed outside the family that require a full array of human capabilities.

37. For more information on the natural advantage of women as fighter pilots, see Linda Bird Francke, *Ground Zero* (New York: Simon and Schuster, 1997), p. 236.

38. Nor does it seem that Rawls could have been referring to this sense of gender roles that is compatible with equal opportunity when he claims

that we "may have to allow for some traditional gendered division of labor within families," because the family roles that would be gender roles in this sense, such as the roles of childbearing and breastfeeding, are not roles over which we "may have to allow for some traditional gendered division of labor." Rather they are roles over which of biological necessity there must be, in this sense, a gendered division of labor.

39. For one of these exceptions working within the Aristotelian tradition, see the work of Martha Nussbaum, most recently *Sex and Social Justice* (New York: Oxford University Press, 1998).

40. See the selections in James P. Sterba, *Ethics: Classical Western Texts in Feminist and Multicultural Perspectives* (New York: Oxford University Press, 1999).

41. A classic feminist discussion of the public/private distinction is Carole Pateman's "Feminist Critiques of the Public/Private Dichotomy," in S. I. Been and G. F. Gaus, eds., *Public and Private in Social Life* (New York: St. Martin's Press, 1983), pp. 281–347.

42. Edmund Morgan, *The Puritan Family* (New York: Harper and Row, 1966), p. 148.

43. Anthony Platt, *The Child Savers: The Invention of Delinquency* (Chicago: University of Chicago Press, 1969), p. 111.

44. See Stephanie Coontz, *The Way We Never Were,* p. 137.

45. Ibid., p. 136.

46. Noreen Connell, "Feminists and Families," *The Nation* (August 1986), pp. 106–8.

47. For further discussion, see my book *Justice for Here and Now,* pp. 93–99.

48. See note 27.

49. Barrie Thorne, *Rethinking the Family* (Boston: Northeastern University Press, 1992), p. 9.

50. Stephanie Coontz, *The Way We Never Were,* chapter 11. There is also considerable evidence that during the heyday of the traditional family—the fifties and sixties in the United States—it was not all that good for women. See Coontz, chapter 3.

51. Francine Blau and Ronald Ehrenberg, eds., *Gender and Family Issues in the Workplace* (New York, Russell Sage Foundation, 1997), p. 1.

52. See *Statistical Abstracts of the United States 1996,* p. 426.

53. For further discussion, see my book *Justice for Here and Now,* pp. 109–12.

54. Lecturing in Leningrad in 1989, my partner, Janet Kourany, and I were told by two male university students that men were by nature incapable of cleaning toilets.

55. Virginia Valian, *Why So Slow?* (Cambridge: MIT Press, 1998), p. 40. What is even more surprising is that married women who work outside the home have similar cutoff points. They do not find the division as unfair to themselves until they are doing about 75 percent of the housework. When they are doing 66 percent of the work they judge the division of housework as fair to both parties.

56. Catharine MacKinnon, *Feminism Unmodified* (Cambridge: Harvard University Press, 1987), chapter 14; *Only Words* (Cambridge: Harvard University Press, 1993), chapter 1. According to MacKinnon, the materials used in the practice of hard-core pornography are sexually explicit, violent, and sexist, and she contrasts them with the materials used in the practice of erotica, which are also sexually explicit but premised on equality. Obviously, though, it is not always easy to classify sexually explicit materials properly.

57. See MacKinnon, *Feminism Unmodified,* chapter 14. See also Andrea Dworkin, *Pornography: Men Possessing Women* (New York: Plume, 1989); Susan Cole, *Pornography and the Sex Crisis* (Toronto: Amanita, 1989); Catharine MacKinnon, *Pornography and Sexual Violence: Evidence of the Links* (London: Everywoman Ltd., 1988).

58. MacKinnon, *Feminism Unmodified,* chapter 14; *Pornography and Sexual Violence* (London: Everywoman Ltd., 1988). See also Gloria Cowan, "Pornography: Conflict Among Feminists," in *Women,* ed. by Jo Freeman, 5th ed. (Mountain View, Calif.: Mayfield, 1995) pp. 347–64; Diana Russell, ed., *Making Violence Sexy* (New York: Teachers College Press, 1993).

59. Franklin Mark Osanka and Sara Lee Johann, *Sourcebook on Pornography* (New York: Lexington Books, 1989).

60. Op. cit.

61. Susan Dwyer, *The Problem of Pornography* (Belmont: Wadsworth Publishing Co., 1995), p. 2.

62. There is also another possibility here. The central purpose of the First Amendment is to protect the speech needed for public deliberation. It can be argued that the "speech" of hard-core pornography is far afield from the speech the First Amendment was designed to protect. For more on this point, see Cass Sunstein, "Feminism and Legal Theory," *Harvard Law Review* (1988), 826–44.

63. *Donald Victor Butler v. Her Majesty the Queen.*

64. For this kind of feminist reaction to hard-core pornography, see Stephanie Bauer, "Pornography, Language and Identity," presented at the 13th International Social Philosophy Conference held in De Pere, Wisconsin, August 15–18, 1996, and forthcoming in the *Proceedings* of the conference.

65. See John Stoltenberg, *Refusing to Be a Man: Essays on Sex and Justice* (Portland, Ore.: Breitenbush Books Inc. 1989), part 3.

66. For a discussion of this and other contexts, see my article "Is Feminism Good for Men and Are Men Good for Feminism?" in Tom Digby, *Men Doing Feminism* (New York: Routledge, 1998), pp. 291–304.

67. *A Theory of Justice,* p. 437.

68. Beverly Walker, "Psychology and Feminism—If You Can't Beat Them, Join Them," in *Men's Studies Modified,* ed. Dale Spender (Oxford: Pergamon Press, 1981), pp. 112–14.

69. Debra Renee Kaufman, "Professional Women: How Real Are the Recent Gains?" in *Feminist Philosophies,* 2nd ed. ed. Janet A. Kourany, James P. Sterba and Rosemarie Tong (Upper Saddle River: Prentice-Hall, 1999), pp. 189–202.

70. On this point, see Edmund Pincoffs, *Quandaries and Virtue* (Lawrence: University of Kansas Press, 1986), chapter 5.

71. For a valuable discussion and critique of these two viewpoints, see Iris Young, "Humanism, Gynocentrism and Feminist Politics," *Women's Studies International Forum* 8 (1985), pp. 173–83.

Chapter 4: Multiculturalism

1. For earlier criticisms of multicultural education in Canada, Australia and Great Britain, see S. Modgil et al., eds., *Multicultural Education: The Interminable Debate* (London: Falmer Press, 1986).

2. John Searle, "The Storm over the University," *New York Review of Books,* December 6, 1990.

3. Dinesh D'Souza, *Illiberal Education* (New York, Vintage Books, 1991), pp. 68–69.

4. Mary Louise Pratt, "Humanities for the Future: Reflections on the Western Culture Debate at Stanford," in *The Politics of Liberal Education,* ed.

Darryl Gless and Barbara Hernstein Smith (Durham: Duke University Press, 1992), p. 25.

5. Ibid.

6. Ibid., p. 15.

7. Richard A. Lanham, "The Extraordinary Convergence: Democracy, Technology, Theory and the University Curriculum," in *The Politics of Liberal Education,* p. 35. See also John Searle, "The Storm over the University," and *U.S. Statistical Abstracts for 1996,* p. 181.

8. See John Garcia, "A Multicultural America: Living in a Sea of Diversity," in Dean Harris, *Multiculturalism from the Margins* (Westport, Conn.: Bergin and Garvey, 1995), pp. 29–38.

9. Now there are other ways to interpret the challenge of multiculturalism to traditional ethics. I have intepreted it as a challenge that comes from non-Western cultures. One might also interpret it as a challenge that comes from, for example, feminist culture, gay and lesbian culture, or class culture. My preference is to treat these other challenges separately since they have often been stressed and I want to give the non-Western challenge the attention it deserves.

10. The will of the majority if it is to be morally legitimate must be backed up with more than power. The minority must have a moral duty to accept the imposition of the majority, but that could only be the case if the minority would be morally blameworthy for failing to accept that imposition.

11. Luke 10:25–37.

12. I am claiming that traditional ethics is biased in favor of Western culture and that to avoid that bias we must engage in a comparable evaluation of Western and non-Western moral ideals, which in turn will require that we take into account the relevant historical and cultural facts needed to interpret and apply those ideals.

13. In chapter 1, I noted that those who endorse a Kantian perspective do not usually formulate it in such a way as would enable it to take nonhuman interests into account.

14. See Annie Booth and Harvery Jacobs, "Ties That Bind: Native American Beliefs as a Foundation for Environmental Consciousness," *Environmental Ethics* 12 (1990), pp. 27–43; Baird Callicott, *Earth's Insights* (Berkeley: University of California Press, 1994), pp. 119–30; Donald Hughes, "Forest Indians: the Holy Occupation," *Environmental Review* 2 (1977), pp. 1–13.

15. Quoted in Warren, "The Power and Promise of Ecological Feminism," in James P. Sterba, ed., *Earth Ethics,* 2nd ed. (Upper Saddle River: Prentice-Hall, 2000).

16. Edward Curtis, *Native American Wisdom* (Philadelphia: Temple University Press, 1993), p. 87.

17. Luther Standing Bear, *Land of the Spotted Eagle* (Boston: Houghton Mifflin, 1933), p. 45.

18. Jorge Valadez, "Pre-Columbian Philosophical Perspectives," in *Ethics: Classical Western Texts in Feminist and Multicultural Perspectives,* ed. James P. Sterba (New York: Oxford University Press, 2000), pp. 106–8.

19. Moshoeshoe II, "Harmony with Nature and Indigenous African Culture," in Sterba, *Ethics,* pp. 527–33.

20. Of course, there is evidence that sometimes American Indians were extraordinarily destructive of their environment, and that while they were respectful of the wildlife that surrounded them, they did not always conserve it, or even see conservation as necessary. But none of this should not stop us from making use of the more positive message from American Indian culture. See Shepard Krech III, *The Ecological Indian* (New York: Norton, 1999).

21. H. G. Creel, *Confucius: The Man and the Myth* (Westport, Conn.: Greenwood Press, 1972).

22. Ibid.

23. Ibid.

24. Ibid.

25. See David Wong, "Community, Diversity, and Confucianism," in *In The Company of Others,* Nancy Snow, ed. (Lanham: Rowman and Littlefield, 1996), pp. 17–37; Russell Fox, "Confucian and Communitarian Responses, *Review of Politics* (1997), pp. 561–92.

26. Maria Eftimiades, "Blood Bond," *People,* August 10, 1998, p. 477.

27. Maxine Hong Kingston, "White Tigers," in *The Woman Warrior* (New York: Knopf, 1977), pp. 17–54.

28. Ward Churchill, "Perversions of Justice: A Native-American Examination of the Doctrine of U.S. Rights to Occupancy in North America," in Sterba, *Ethics,* pp. 401–18.

29. Ibid.

30. Michael Apple, *Official Knowledge* (New York: Routledge, 1993), p. 65.

31. David Stannard, *American Holocaust* (New York: Oxford University Press, 1992), pp. 261–68; Lenore Stiffarm with Phil Lane Jr., "The Demography of Native North America," in *The State of Native America,* ed., Annette Jaimes, (Boston: South End Press, 1992), pp. 23ff.

32. Dee Brown, *Bury My Heart at Wounded Knee* (New York: Holt, 1970), p. 1.

33. Stannard, pp. 74–75.

34. These diseases included smallpox, measles, bubonic plague, diphtheria, influenza, malaria, yellow fever, and typhoid.

35. Bartolome De Las Casas, *The Devastation of the Indies,* trans. Herma Briffault (Baltimore: John Hopkins University Press, 1974), p. 78.

36. Ibid., pp. 33–34.

37. Stannard, pp. 70–71.

38. Ibid., p. 85.

39. Ibid., pp. 75–76.

40. Las Casas, p. 51. One castellano was the equivalent of 4.5 grams of gold.

41. Ibid., p. 51.

42. Ibid., pp. 110, 125.

43. Stannard, pp. 87–89.

44. Ibid., p. 95.

45. Ibid., p. 106.

46. Ibid., p. 119.

47. Ibid., p. 120.

48. Richard Drinnon, *Facing West: The Metaphysics of Indian Hating and Empire Building* (Minneapolis: University of Minnesota Press, 1980), pp. 331–32.

49. Ibid., p. 332.

50. Lenore Stiffarm with Phil Lane Jr., p. 32; Ward Churchill, *Indians Are Us?* (Monroe: Common Courage Press, 1994), chapter 1.

51. Stannard, pp. 121ff.

52. Ibid., p. 122. Michael Paul Rogin, *Fathers and Children: Andrew Jackson and the Subjugation of the American Indians* (New York: Knopf, 1975), p. 227.

53. Stannard, p. 131.

54. Brown, p. 170.

55. Stannard, p. 245.

56. Ibid; William Dean Howells, "A Sennight of the Contennial," *Atlantic Monthly* 38 (July 1876), p. 103.

57. Quoted in Thomas G. Dyer, *Theodore Roosevelt and the Idea of Race* (Baton Rouge: Louisiana State University Press, 1980), p. 78.

58. Churchill, p. 37.

59. Lenore Stiffarm with Phil Lane Jr., p. 36.

60. Sharon O'Brien, *American Tribal Governments* (Norman: University of Oklahoma Press, 1989), p. 76.

61. Ibid.

62. Stannard, pp. 256–57.

63. O'Brien, p. 77.

64. Stannard, p. 257.

65. Ibid., p. 3.

66. Stannard, pp. 62, 202.

67. See Adolf Hitler, *Hitler's Secret Book,* trans. Salvator Attanasio (New York: Grove Press, 1961), pp. 44–48.

68. Roger Manvell and Heinrich Fraenkel, *The Incomparable Crime* (New York: Putnam, 1967), p. 45.

69. See Ward Churchill, "A Summary of Arguments Against the Naming of a University Residence After Clinton M. Tyler," quoted in Annette Jaimes, "Introduction," *The State of Native America,* p. 4.

70. For example, in the title of David Stannard's book.

71. Ward Churchill, *The Struggle for the Land* (Monroe: Common Courage Press, 1993), part 4. The following discussion is based on this book.

72. George Moss, *Vietnam: An American Ordeal*, 3rd ed., (Upper Saddle River: Prentice-Hall, 1990), chapter 1; Ronald Cima, ed., *Vietnam: A Country Study* (Washington D.C.: Library of Congress, 1987), chapter 1; Neil Sheehan, *A Bright Shining Lie* (New York: Random House, 1988), book 2; Michael Charlton and Anthony Moncrieff, *Many Reasons Why: The American Involvement in Vietnam* (New York: Hill and Wang, 1978), chapter 1; Stanley Karnow, *Vietnam: A History* (New York: Viking, 1991), chapter 3.

73. George Moss, *A Vietnam Reader* (Upper Saddle River: Prentice-Hall, 1991), pp. 32–34.

74. Sheehan, book 2; Karnow, chapter 3.

75. Ibid.; Moss, *Vietnam: An American Ordeal*, chapter 1; Charlton and Moncrieff, chapter 1; Karnow, chapter 3.

76. Sheehan, book 2.

77. See Sandra Taylor, "Vietnam in the Beginning," *Reviews in American History* (1989), p. 308.

78. George Herring, "The Vietnam Analogy and the 'Lessons' of History," in *The Vietnam War as History*, ed. Elizabeth Errington and B. J. C. McKercher (New York: Praeger, 1990), pp. 3–15; Karnow, chapter 1.

79. Moss, *Vietnam*, chapter 1; Sheehan, book 2; Cima, Chapter 1; Karnow, Chapter 2.

80. Moss, *Vietnam*, chapter 1; Sheehan, book 2; Karnow, Chapter 2.

81. Ibid.; Cima, Chapter 1; Karnow, Chapter 2.

82. Sheehan, book 2.

83. Moss, *Vietnam*, chapter 1; Sheehan, book 2; Karnow, chapter 3.

84. George McT. Kahin, "The Origins of U.S. Involvement in Vietnam" in *The Vietnam War as History*, ed. Elizabeth Errington and B. J. C. McKercher, p. 62; Sheehan, book 2; Karnow, chapter 3.

85. Moss, *Vietnam*, chapter 2; Cima, chapter 1; Sheehan, book 2; Karnow, chapter 3.

Chapter 5: Conclusion

1. Quoted from Deborah Tannen, *The Argument Culture* (New York: Basic Books, 1998), p. 54. Tannen's book is an excellent discussion of the prevalence of warmaking strategy in modern culture.

2. Quoted from Monroe Friedman, "Kinder, Gentler, But Not So Zealous," *The Recorder*, August 23, 1995.

3. Charles Yablon, "Stupid Lawyer Tricks," *Columbia Law Review* (1996), p. 1618.

4. This case is discussed in Tannen, pp. 152–53.

5. Jonathan Harr, *A Civil Action* (New York: Vintage Books, 1995).

6. It is also important to distinguish doing philosophy in the sense of establishing philosophical conclusions before one's philosophical peers from doing philosophy in the sense of teaching or explaining philosophy to stu-

dents and nonphilosophers. Here I am primarily concerned with doing philosophy in this first sense.

7. For a discussion of the similarities between argument and war, see George Lakoff and Mark Johnson, *Metaphors We Live By* (Chicago: University of Chicago Press, 1980), pp. 4–6, 77–86; Edwin Burtt, "Philosophers as Warriors," in *The Critique of War,* ed. Robert Ginsberg (Chicago: Regnery, 1969), pp. 30–42. Lakoff and Johnson argue that these similarities between argument and war are constitutive features of the nature of argument.

8. In *Justice for Here and Now,* I set out an earlier version of this peacemaking way of doing philosophy and apply it to the area of social and political philosophy.

9. Although names are omitted, the events described in this chapter actually did occur.

10. See William James, *The Moral Equivalent of War* (Association for International Conciliation, 1910); John Stuart Mill, *On Liberty* (New York: Bobbs-Merrill, 1956). The phrase "marketplace of ideas" is associated with Mill's work but surprisingly the phrase never appears in his writings and, in fact, is somewhat at odds with the views he actually endorsed. See Jill Gordon, "John Stuart Mill and the 'Marketplace of Ideas,' " *Social Theory and Practice* 23 (1997).

11. This does not happen only in philosophy. In an article in *The New York Times,* Lester Thurow and Paul Krugman, both at MIT and known for their opposing economic views, were said to "go at it, *never face to face,* always in writing and public speaking, sometimes from the well of the same MIT lecture amphitheater, although on separate days . . ." (emphasis added). *New York Times,* February 16, 1997.

12. A number of these papers can be found in the 1960 and 1961 issues of *Philosophical Studies.*

13. Data on the profession, APA Website.

14. Bernice R. Sander, "The Campus Climate Revisited: Chilly for Women Faculty, Administrators, and Graduate Students" (Washington, D.C.: Association of American Colleges, October 1986); Roberta Hall and Bernice Sander, "The Classroom Climate: A Chilly One for Women" (Ibid., October 1982); Hall and Sander, "Out of the Classroom: A Chilly Campus Climate for Women" (Ibid., October 1984).

BIBLIOGRAPHY

Apple, Michael. *Official Knowledge* (New York: Routledge, 1993).

Arneson, Richard. "Feminism and Family Justice," *Public Affairs Quarterly* 11: 4, October 1997, pp. 318–19.

Attfield, Robin. *The Ethics of Environmental Concern* (New York: Columbia University Press, 1983).

Blau, Francine, and Ronald Ehrenberg, eds. *Gender and Family Issues in the Workplace* (New York: Russell Sage Foundation, 1997).

Booth, Annie, and Harvey Jacobs. "Ties that Bind: Native American Beliefs as a Foundation for Environmental Consciousness," *Environmental Ethics* 12 (1990), pp. 27–43.

Brown, Dee. *Bury My Heart at Wounded Knee* (New York: Holt, 1970).

Callicott, Baird. "Animal Liberation: A Triangular Affair," *Environmental Ethics* 2 (1980), pp. 311–28.

———. *In Defense of the Land Ethic* (Albany: State University Press of New York, 1989).

———. *Earth's Insights* (Berkeley: University of California Press, 1994).

Card, Claudia, ed. *Feminist Ethics* (Lawrence: University of Kansas Press, 1991).

———. "Particular Justice and General Care," in *Controversies in Feminism,* ed. James P. Sterba (Lanham: Rowman and Littlefield, 2000).

Causey, Ann. "On the Morality of Hunting," *Environmental Ethics* (1989), pp. 327–43.

Charlton, Michael, and Anthony Moncrieff, *Many Reasons Why: The American Involvement in Vietnam* (New York: Hill and Wang, 1978).

Chodorow, Nancy. *Mothering: Psychoanalysis and the Sociology of Gender* (Berkeley: University of California Press, 1978).

Churchill, Ward. *The Struggle for the Land* (Monroe: Common Courage Press, 1993).

———. *Indians Are Us?* (Monroe: Common Courage Press, 1994).

———. "Perversions of Justice: A Native-American Examination of the Doctrine of U.S. Rights to Occupancy in North America," in *Ethics: Classical Western Texts in Feminist and Multicultural Perspectives,* ed. James P. Sterba (New York: Oxford University Press, 2000), pp. 401–18.

Cima, Ronald, ed. *Vietnam: A Country Study* (Washington, D.C.: Library of Congress, 1987).

Cole, Eve Browning, and Susan Coultrap-McQuin, eds. *Exploration in Feminist Ethics* (Bloomington: Indiana University Press, 1992).

Cole, Susan. *Pornography and the Sex Crisis* (Toronto: Amanita, 1989).

Connell, Noreen. "Feminists and Families," *The Nation* (1986), pp. 106–8.

Coontz, Stephanie. *The Way We Never Were* (New York: Basic Books, 1992).

Cost, Quality and Child Outcomes Study Team. *Cost, Quality and Child Outcomes in Child Care Centers,* 2nd ed. (Denver: University of Colorado Press, 1995).

Costello, Cynthia, and Anne Stone. *The American Woman 1994–95* (New York: Norton, 1994).

Coverman, Shelley. "Women's Work is Never Done," in *Women: A Feminist Perspective,* 4th ed. ed. Jo Freeman (Mountain View, Calif.: Mayfield, 1989), pp. 356–68.

Cowan, Gloria. "Pornography: Conflict Among Feminists" in *Women,* edited by Jo Freeman, Fifth Edition. (Mountain View, Calif.: Mayfield, 1995), pp. 347–64.

Creel, H. G. *Confucius: The Man and the Myth* (Westport, Conn.: Greenwood Press, 1972).

Curtis, Edward. *Native American Wisdom* (Philadelphia: Temple University Press, 1993).

De Las Casas, Bartolome. *The Devastation of the Indies*, trans. Herma Briffault (Baltimore: Johns Hopkins University Press, 1974).

Dinnerstein, Dorothy. *The Mermaid and the Minotaur* (New York: Harper and Row, 1977).

Drinnon, Richard. *Facing West: The Metaphysics of Indian Hating and Empire Building* (Minneapolis: University of Minnesota Press, 1980).

D'Souza, Dinesh. *Illiberal Education* (New York: Vintage Books, 1991).

Dworkin, Andrea. *Pornography: Men Possessing Women* (New York: Plume, 1989).

Dwyer, Susan. *The Problem of Pornography* (Belmont, Wadsworth, 1995).

Etzioni, Amitai, *The Spirit of Community* (Crown, 1993).

England, Paula, ed. *Theory on Gender/Feminism on Theory* (New York: Aldine De Gruyter, 1993).

English, Deirdre. "Through the Glass Ceiling," *Mother Jones,* November 1992.

Faludi, Susan. *Backlash* (New York: Crown, 1988).

Ferguson, Ann. "Androgyny as an Ideal for Human Development," in *Feminism and Philosophy,* ed. Mary Vetterling-Braggin et al. (Totowa: Rowman and Littlefield, 1977), pp. 45–69.

Flynn, Eileen. *Cradled in Human Hands* (Kansas City: Sheed and Ward, 1991).

Fox, Russell. "Confucian and Communitarian Responses," *The Review of Politics* (1997), pp. 561–92.

Friedman, Monroe. "Kinder, Gentler, But Not So Zealous," *The Recorder,* August 23, 1995.

Garcia, John. "A Multicultural America: Living in a Sea of Diversity,"in Dean Harris, *Multiculturalism from the Margins* (Westport, Conn.: Bergin and Garvey, 1995), pp. 29–38.

Gewirth, Alan. "The Non-Trivializability of Universalizability," *Australasian Journal of Philosophy* (1969), pp. 123–31.

Gilligan, Carol. *In a Different Voice* (Cambridge: Harvard University Press, 1982).

———. Moral Orientations and Moral Development," in *Women and Moral Theory*, ed. Eva Kittay and Diana Meyers (Totowa: Rowman and Littlefield, 1987).

Grimshaw, Jean. *Philosophy and Feminist Thinking* (Minneapolis: University of Minnesota Press, 1986).

Gruzalski, Bart. "The Case against Raising and Killing Animals for Food" in H. Miller and W. Williams, *Ethics and Animals* (Clifton N.J.: Humana Press, 1983), pp. 251–63.

Hargrove, Eugene. *Foundations of Environmental Ethics* (Englewood Cliffs: Prentice Hall, 1989).

Harr, Jonathan. *A Civil Action* (New York: Vintage Books, 1995).

Held, Virginia, ed. *Justice and Care* (Boulder: Westview, 1995).

———. "Caring Relations and Principles of Justice" in *Controversies in Feminism*, ed. James P. Sterba (Lanham: Rowman and Littlefield, 2000).

Herring, George. "The Vietnam Analogy and the 'Lessons' of History," in *The Vietnam War as History,* ed. Elizabeth Errington and B. J. C. McKercher (New York: Praeger, 1990), pp. 3–15.

Hersch, Joni, and Leslie Stratton. "Housework, Wages, and the Division of Housework Time for Employed Spouses," *AEA Papers and Proceedings* 84 (1994), pp. 120–25.

Hughes, Donald. "Forest Indians: The Holy Occupation," *Environmental Review* 2 (1977), pp. 1–13.

Jamieson, Dale. "Rights, Justice and Duties to Provide Assistance: A Critique of Regan's Theory of Rights," *Ethics* (1990), pp. 349–62.

Johnson, Lawrence. *A Morally Deep World* (New York: Cambridge University Press, 1991).

———. "Toward the Moral Considerability of Species and Ecosystems," *Environmental Ethics* 14 (1992), pp. 145–51.

Kahin, George McT. "The Origins of U.S. Involvement in Vietnam" in *The Vietnam War as History*, ed. by Elizabeth Errington and B. J. C. McKercher, pp. 57–72.

Kalin, Jesse. "In Defense of Egoism," in *Morality and Rational Self-Interest*, ed. David Gauthier (Englewood Cliffs: Prentice-Hall, 1970), pp. 73–74.

Kamerman, Sheila. "Starting Right: What We Owe Our Children Under Three," *The American Prospect*, Winter 1991.

Karnow, Stanley. *Vietnam: A History* (New York: Viking, 1991).

Kaufman, Debra Renee. "Professional Women: How Real Are the Recent Gains?" in *Feminist Philosophies*, 2nd ed. ed. Janet A. Kourany, James P. Sterba and Rosemarie Tong (Upper Saddle River: Prentice-Hall, 1999), pp. 189–202.

Koehn, Daryl. *Rethinking Feminist Ethics* (New York: Routledge, 1998).

Krech, Shepard, III. *The Ecological Indian* (New York: Norton, 1999).

Kymlicka, Will. *Contemporary Political Philosophy* (New York: Oxford University Press, 1990).

Lanham, Richard A. "The Extraordinary Convergence: Democracy, Technology, Theory and the University Curriculum," in *The Politics of Liberal Education*, pp. 33–56.

Lappe, Frances Moore, and Joseph Collins. *Food First* (Boston: Houghton Mifflin, 1977).

Lappe, Frances Moore. *Diet for a Small Planet* (New York: Ballantine Books, 1982) p. 69.

———. *World Hunger* (Grove Press, 1986).

Larrabee, Mary Jeanne. "Feminism and Parental Roles: Possibilities for Changes," *Journal of Social Philosophy* 14 (1983), pp. 16–22.

Leopold, Aldo. *A Sand County Almanac* (Oxford: Oxford University Press, 1949).

Lindsey, Linda. *Gender Roles* (Englewood Cliffs: Prentice Hall, 1990).

Lloyd, Sharon. "Situating a Feminist Criticism of John Rawls's *Political Liberalism*," *Loyola of Los Angeles Law Review* 28 (1995), pp. 1338–43.

Lorbor, Judith. *Paradoxes of Gender* (New Haven: Yale University Press, 1994).

Luce, R. Duncan, and Howard Raiffa. *Games and Decisions* (New York: John Wiley, 1967).

MacKinnon, Catharine. *Feminism Unmodified* (Cambridge: Harvard University Press, 1987).

———. *Pornography and Sexual Violence: Evidence of the Links* (London: Everywoman Ltd., 1988).

———. *Only Words* (Cambridge: Harvard University Press, 1993).

Manvell, Roger, and Heinrich Fraenkel. *The Incomparable Crime* (New York: Putnam, 1967).

Miller, G. Tyler Jr. *Living With the Environment* (Belmont: Wadsworth, 1990).

Modgil, Sohan, et al., eds. *Multicultural Education: The Interminable Debate* (London: Falmer Press, 1986).

Moen, Phyllis. *Woman's Two Roles* (New York: Auburn House, 1992).

Morgan, Edmund. *The Puritan Family* (New York: Harper and Row, 1966).

Moshoeshoe II. "Harmony with Nature and Indigenous African Culture," in *Ethics: Classical Western Texts in Feminist and Multicultural Perspectives,* ed. James P. Sterba (New York: Oxford University Press, 2000), pp. 527–33.

Moss, George. *Vietnam: An American Ordeal,* 3rd ed. (Upper Saddle River: Prentice-Hall, 1990).

———. *A Vietnam Reader* (Upper Saddle River: Prentice-Hall, 1991).

Moulton, Janice. "A Paradigm of Philosophy: The Adversary Method," in *Discovering Reality,* ed. by Sandra Harding and Merrill B. Hintikka (Dordrecht: Reidel, 1983), pp. 149–64.

Nelson, Hilde Lindemann, ed. *Feminism and Families,* (New York: Routledge, 1997).

Nodding, Nell. *Caring: A Feminine Approach to Ethics and Moral Education* (Berkeley: University of California Press, 1984).

Nussbaum, Martha. *Sex and Social Justice* (New York: Oxford University Press, 1998).

O'Brien, Sharon. *American Tribal Governments* (Norman: University of Oklahoma Press, 1989).

Okin, Susan. *Justice, Gender and the Family* (New York: Basic Books, 1989).

———. "Feminism and Political Philosophy," *Philosophy in a Different Voice,* ed. Janet Kourany (Princeton: Princeton University Press, 1997), pp. 116–44.

Osanka, Franklin Mark, and Sara Lee Johann. *Sourcebook on Pornography* (New York: Lexington Books, 1989).

Pateman, Carole. "Feminist Critiques of the Public/Private Dichotomy," in S. I. Been and G. F. Gaus, eds., *Public and Private in Social Life* (New York: St. Martin's Press, 1983), pp. 281–347.

Platt, Anthony. *The Child Savers: The Invention of Delinquency* (Chicago: University of Chicago Press, 1969).

Pratt, Mary Louise. "Humanities for the Future: Reflections on the Western Culture Debate at Stanford," in *The Politics of Liberal Education,* eds. Darryl Gless and Barbara Herrnstein Smith (Durham: Duke University Press, 1992), pp. 13–31.

Rawls, John. *A Theory of Justice* (Cambridge: Harvard University Press, 1971).

————. *Political Liberalism* (New York: Columbia University Press, 1993).

————. "The Idea of Public Reason Revisited," *University of Chicago Law Review* (1997), pp. 787–94.

Regan, Tom. *The Case for Animal Rights* (Berkeley: University of California Press, 1983).

Rogin, Michael Paul. *Fathers and Children: Andrew Jackson and the Subjugation of the American Indians* (New York: Knopf, 1975).

Rolston, Holmes. *Environmental Ethics* (Philadelphia: Temple University Press, 1988).

Russell, Diana, ed. *Making Violence Sexy* (New York: Teachers College Press, 1993).

Sagoff, Mark. "Animal Liberation and Environmental Ethics: Bad Marriage, Quick Divorce," *Osgood Hall Law Journal* 22 (1984), pp. 297–307.

Sapontzis, S. F. *Morals, Reason and Animals* (Philadelphia: Temple University Press, 1987).

Searle, John. "The Storm over the University," *New York Review of Books*, December 6, 1990.

Sheehan, Neil. *A Bright Shining Lie* (New York: Randon House, 1988).

Sidel, Ruth. "Day Care: Do We Really Care?" in *Issues in Feminism,* ed. Sheila Ruth (Mountain View, Calif.: Mayfield, 1990), pp. 336–45.

Singer, Marcus. *Generalization in Ethics* (New York: Knopf, 1961).

Singer, Peter. *Animal Liberation* (New York: Avon, 1975).

————. *Practical Ethics* (Cambridge: Cambridge University Press, 1979).

Stace, W. T. *The Concept of Morals* (New York: MacMillian, 1937).

Standing Bear, Luther. *Land of the Spotted Eagle* (Boston: Houghton Mifflin, 1933).

Stannard, David. *American Holocaust* (New York: Oxford University Press, 1992).

Steffen, Lloyd. "In Defense of Dominion," *Environmental Ethics* 14 (1992), pp. 63–80.

Sterba, James P.,"Ethical Egoism and Beyond," *Canadian Journal of Philosophy* (1979), pp. 91–108.

————. *The Demands of Justice* (Notre Dame: University of Notre Dame Press, 1980).

————. *How to Make People Just* (Totowa: Rowman and Littlefield, 1988).

————. "Response to Nine Commentators," *Journal of Social Philosophy* 22 (1991), pp. 100–118.

————. "Reconciling Conceptions of Justice," in James P. Sterba et al., *Morality and Social Justice* (Lanham: Rowman and Littlefield, 1994), pp. 1–38.

————. "Reconciling Anthropocentric and Nonanthropocentric Environmental Ethics," *Environmental Values* (1994) pp. 229–44.

————. *Contemporary Social and Political Philosophy* (Belmont: Wadsworth, 1995).

————. *Social and Political Philosophy: Classical Western Texts in Feminist and Multicultural Perspectives,* 2nd ed. (Belmont: Wadsworth, 1997).

————. "A Biocentrist Fights Back," *Environmental Ethics* (Winter 1998), pp. 361–76.

————. "Is Feminism Good for Men and Are Men Good for Feminism?" in Tom Digby, *Men Doing Feminism* (New York: Routledge, 1998), pp. 291–304.

————. *Justice for Here and Now* (New York: Cambridge University Press, 1998).

————. "Response to Five Commentators," *Journal of Social Philosophy* 30 (1999), pp. 424–37.

————. *Earth Ethics,* 2nd ed. (Upper Saddle River: Prentice-Hall, 2000).

————. *Ethics: Classical Western Texts in Feminist and Multicultural Perspectives* (New York: Oxford University Press, 2000).

Stiffarm, Lenore, with Phil Lane, Jr. "The Demography of Native North America," in *The State of Native America,* ed. Annette Jaimes (Boston: South End Press, 1992), pp. 23–54.

Stoltenberg, John. *Refusing to Be a Man: Essays on Sex and Justice* (Portland, Ore.: Breitenbush, 1989).

Sunstein, Cass. "Feminism and Legal Theory," *Harvard Law Review* (1988), pp. 826–44.

Tannen, Dehorah. *You Just Don't Understand* (New York: Ballantine Books, 1990).

————. *The Argument Culture* (New York: Basic Books, 1998).

Taylor, Paul. *Respect for Nature* (Princeton: Princeton University Press, 1987).

Taylor, Sandra. "Vietnam in the Beginning," *Reviews in American History* (1989), p. 308.

Thorne, Barrie. *Rethinking the Family* (Boston: Northeastern University Press, 1992).

Valadez, Jorge. "Pre-Columbian Philosophical Perspectives," in *Ethics: Classical Western Texts in Feminist and Multicultural Perspectives,* ed. James P. Sterba (New York: Oxford University Press, 2000), pp. 106–8.

Valian, Virginia. *Why So Slow?* (Cambridge: MIT Press, 1998).

Walker, Beverly. "Psychology and Feminism—If You Can't Beat Them, Join Them," in *Men's Studies Modified,* ed. Dale Spender (Oxford: Pergamon Press, 1981), pp. 111–24.

Warren, Karen. "The Power and Promise of EcoFeminism," *Environmental Ethics* 12 (1990), pp. 121–46.

Warren, Mary Ann. "The Rights of the Nonhuman World," in *Environmental Philosophy,* ed. Robert Elliot and Arran Gare (University Park: Penn State University Press, 1983), pp. 109–34.

————. *Moral Status* (New York: Oxford University Press, 1997).

Weitzman, Lenore. *The Divorce Revolution: The Unexpected Social and Economic Consequences for Women and Children in America* (New York: Free Press, 1985).

White, Lynn. "The Historical Roots of Our Ecological Crisis," *Science* 155 (1967), pp. 1203–7.

Women's Action Coalition. *WAC Stats: the Facts about Women* (New York: New Press, 1993).

Wong, David. "Community, Diversity, and Confucianism," in *In The Company of Others,* ed. Nancy Snow (Lanham: Rowman and Littlefield, 1996), pp. 17–37.

Yablon, Charles. "Stupid Lawyer Tricks," *Columbia Law Review* (1996), pp. 1618–44.

Young, Iris. "Humanism, Gynocentrism and Feminist Politics," *Women's Studies International Forum* 8 (1985), pp. 173–83.

INDEX

Accessibility, 3–4, 78–80
Altruism and the justification of
    morality, 11–19, 120 n.14
Altruistic forbearance, 36, 127 n.46
American Indian culture, 81–83
Androgyny, 74–75, 105
Animal experimentation, 27
Animal libertationists, 27–29,
    40–43
Animals
    farm, 27, 40–42
    wild, 42
Aristotelian ethics, 20–25, 62,
    72–75, 78, 81
Arneson, Richard, 61

Baier, Kurt, 113
Basic needs, 34, 126 n.34
Biocentric individualism, 29–30
Biocentric pluralism, 30–49, 123
    n.7

Callicott, Baird, 40
Cannibalism, 35–36
Card, Claudia, 53–55
Care perspective, 51–55
Cherokee nation, 91–92
Chivington, Colonel John, 92
Churchill, Ward, 87, 94–97
Civil Action, A (Harr), 108
Clinton, Bill, 106–7
Columbus, Christopher, 87–88,
    94
Confucius, 84–87
Cortes, Hernando, 89

Day care, 57–62, 64–67
Divorce law, 64

Egoism
    individual ethical, 6–7
    and justification of morality,
        11–9, 120 n.14
    universal ethical, 7–10
Environmentalism, definition of,
    119 n.1
Equal opportunity, 58–62, 65–71
Erotica, 69

Fact/value gap, 45–47
Factory farming, 27, 40–42
Family
    gendered, 57–62, 105
    traditional, 64–65
Flexible work schedules, 59

Gaip. *See* Vo Nguyen Giap
Gender roles, 57–62, 72–75, 133
    n.38
Genesis, 47–48, 83
Gilligan, Carol, 51–55, 75
God, 124 n.11

Held, Virginia, 53–55
Himmler, Heinrich, 94
Hitler, Adolf, 94
Ho Chi Minh, 97–98, 101–2
Holmes, Oliver Wendel, 92
Holocaust, comparison to conquest
    of the American Indians,
    93–94

Housekeeping and childrearing,
    equal sharing of, 59–63, 65–67
Howells, William Dean, 92
Human-centered environmental
    ethics, 48–49, 130 n.70

Is/ought gap, 45–47

Jackson, Andrew, 91–92
James, William 111
Jefferson, Thomas, 91
Johnson, Lawrence, 123 nn. 6 and 7
Justice and the family, 51–67
Justice perspective, 51–55

Kantian environmentalism, 28–49,
    71–72
Kantian ethics, 21–25, 55–62,
    72–75, 78, 81, 105
Kingston, Maxine Hong, 86–87

Las Casas, Bartolome De, 88–90
Le Loi, 100–101
Leopold, Aldo, 126 n.39
Libertarianism, 41–42, 126 nn. 35
    and 36
Lipstadt, Deborah, 106–7
Lloyd, Sharon, 59–61

MacKinnon, Catharine, 67–69
Mill, John Stuart, 111
Morality as compromise, 14–19
Moshoeshoe II, 82

Ngo Quyen, 99
Nguyen Hue, 100
Non-question-begging
    and the justification of environ-
        mental ethics, 30–32, 124 n.17
    and the justification of morality
        over egoism and altruism,
        11–19
Nussbaum, Martha, 132 n.20, 134,
    n.39

"Oughts" of competitive games,
    9–10

Parental leave, paid and unpaid,
    59–62, 66–67
Particularist perspective, 54–55
Peacemaking way of doing philoso-
    phy, 111–17
Pizarro, Francisco, 90
Popper, Frank and Deborah, 96
Pornography, hard-core, 67–71, 135
    n.62
Practical requirements, problem of,
    19–25
Principle of Disproportionality,
    37–89, 105, 126 n.37
Principle of Human Defense, 33–49,
    105
Principle of Human Preservation,
    34–49, 105, 125 n.28
Principle of Restitution, 38–49, 105
Public/private distinction, 62–71,
    105

Rationality, problem of, 5–19
Rawls, John, 21, 55–62, 71–72, 133
    n.38
Regan, Tom, 28–29, 42–43
Relativism, problem of, 2–5
Roosevelt, Franklin, 98

Sabato, Larry, 106
Sagoff, Mark, 40
Secular ethics, 79–80, 105
Sexual harassment, 94
Sheridan, General Philip, 92
Simpson, Alan, 106
Singer, Peter, 27–28, 42–43
Socialism, 41–42
Starr, Kenneth, 108
Sunstein, Cass, 133 n.62

Taylor, Paul, 29–44
Tran Hung, 100

Trieu Da, 98–99
Trung sisters, 98–99

Universalist perspective, 54–55
Utilitarian environmentalism,
    27–28, 42–43
Utilitarian ethics, 19–25, 62,
    72–77, 78, 81

Valadez, Jorge, 82
Vegetarian diet, 40–42

Viet Minh, 97–98, 102
Vietnam, 97–103
Vo Nguyen Giap, General,
    102

Warmaking way of doing philoso-
    phy, 108–15
Warren, Mary Ann, 40
Washington, George, 91
Welfare liberalism, 41–42
Wu-ti, 99

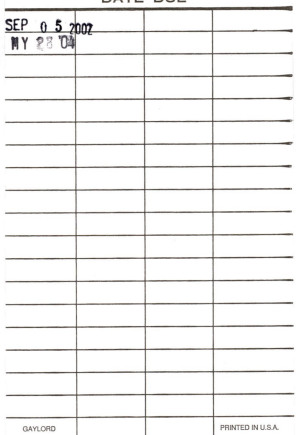

DATE DUE

SEP 0 5 2002			
MY 28 '04			
GAYLORD			PRINTED IN U.S.A.